PEDAL CARS

LARRY BLOEMKER
ROBERT GENAT
ED WEIRICK

MBI Publishing Company

ACKNOWLEDGMENTS

I would like to acknowledge the work of Ed Weirick, without whose expertise this project would not have been possible. A debt of gratitude also goes to my parents, who not only bought me my first pedal car, but didn't question me when I ran it into the side of our home. I was just driving along minding my own business, and the house jumped out in front of me. That's my story, and I'm sticking to it.
—Larry Bloemker

For all of their help, I would like to give special thanks to Ted and Peggy Fleetwood; Craig, Donna, and Garrett Fleetwood; John, Sue, and Darrel Smith.
—Robert Genat

First published in 1999 by MBI Publishing Company, 729 Prospect Avenue, PO Box 1, Osceola, WI 54020-0001 USA

© Larry Bloemker, Robert Genat, Ed Weirick, 1999

MBI Publishing Company books are also available at discounts in bulk quantity for industrial or sales-promotional use. For details write to Special Sales Manager at Motorbooks International Wholesalers & Distributors, 729 Prospect Avenue, P.O. Box 1, Osceola, WI 54020-0001 USA.

Library of Congress Cataloging-in-Publication Data

Bloemker, Larry
    Pedal cars/Larry Bloemker, Robert Genat & Ed Weirick,
        p. cm.
    Includes index.
    ISBN 0-7603-0443-2 (pbk.: alk. paper)
    1. Pedal cars—History. I. Title.
TL483.B56   1999
688.7'28—dc21   99-34754

On the Front Cover: Made between 1941 and 1950, the Murray Pontiac has been a perennial favorite.
On the Frontispiece: Although interesting and attractive, this hood ornament is incorrect on the Steelcraft Oldsmobile. *Zone Five*
On the Title Page: A beautiful illustration of the Murray U.S. Pursuit Plane.
On the Back Cover: (Clockwise from top left) A 1950s IH-Farmall tractor from Eska *Zone Five*; Hamilton's 1959 Chevrolet Kiddybird; Murray's Pursuit Plane was made between 1941 and 1950 *Zone Five*; Murray's Deluxe Pontiac wagon with canopy was produced from 1941 to 1950.

Edited by Jane Mausser
Designed by Tom Heffron

Printed in Hong Kong

CONTENTS

Chapter One

THE CAR IS BORN AND PEDAL CARS FOLLOW

When the automobile made its entry in the late 1800s from pioneering auto makers such as Duryea and Daimler, everyone noticed. Considering the noise and smoke these early cars often produced, people couldn't help but notice. Some scoffed at the idea that these crude machines could replace the horse as a means of effective, personal transportation. Others proclaimed that the automobile would soon change people's lives forever. Not everyone agreed on the impact the automobile would have on everyday life, but everyone did notice.

Given the public fascination and debate over the automobile, it didn't take too long for toy makers to take note of the automobile as well. Throughout history adult items have been reproduced in smaller scale as children's toys. Early craftsmen's efforts at reproducing the automobile for children became what we know today as the pedal car. Often quieter and certainly more reliable than the real cars of the day, the pedal car was a self-powered, miniature version of the automobile.

Wheeled toys such as the tricycle (originally called a velocipede), the bicycle, and wagon had already been introduced; the pedal car was a natural evolution of these designs. By combining the four wheels and wide

The Gendron Company began in 1872, merged with American National Corp. in 1927, and was purchased by the Howe Company in 1964. It is still in business. The company was at its most prosperous in the 1920s when the Pioneer Line was world-famous.

This image from a European postcard shows a very rare pedal car, vintage 1908 to 1914. Today it would fetch $12,000 or more.

7

wheelbase of the wagon with the pedal configurations and steering systems from velocipedes and bicycles and adding a body, the pedal car was born.

These early pedal cars were powered by two basic drive mechanisms: chain drive and pedal power. The chain drive consisted of a front sprocket, to which pedals were attached, and a chain running from the front sprocket to a fixed sprocket on the rear axle that would transfer the power to the rear wheels of the car. Pedal power used a pair of pedals with long levers attached to the rear axle. The rider's legs pumped back and forth to provide power. A little later in the evolution of the pedal car, ball bearings, which were cutting-edge technology in the early twentieth century, were added to make the cars easier to power.

One of the most fascinating aspects of pedal cars is the way they faithfully mimicked the real cars of the day in both styling and production methods. Like the real automobiles that inspired them, the first generation of pedal cars were made for the wealthy. They were individually crafted, simple designs that often lacked fenders and featured iron-spoked wheels like those used on early bicycles. Often built entirely of wood, early pedal cars featured designs based on the horseless carriage. Some even featured a tiller steering mechanism as opposed to a steering wheel. Higher quality examples had wood frames with surrounding metal panels. The metal frame was introduced after the turn of the century. Because these were usually expensive children's toys, many pedal cars featured impressive detailing such as horns, hand brakes, and even oil lamps to provide illumination for rides that were likely to take place past their owner's bedtime.

In the years following 1900, the horseless carriage experienced a dramatic transformation. Breakthroughs in engine design, steering, and braking caused detractors of the automobile to stop doubting its usefulness and start mourning the passing of the horse as a staple of American life. In 1908 Henry Ford introduced his famous Model T. Built from a strong steel alloy and powered by a four-cylinder engine that reached

The early velocipede, or tricycle, pictured here in a drawing from 1886, was the first adult vehicle from which a small child's version was copied. The child's model, like the adult's, was propelled by means of treadles attached to cranks or levers.

a cruising speed of 25 miles per hour, the Model T was created to provide affordable transportation for middle-class America. At $850 the "Tin Lizzy," as the Model T came to be known, helped put America on wheels.

With the automobile well on its way to carving out a place in modern life, the pedal car soon followed suit. Pedal car manufacturers were quick to add the famous automobile names of the day to their offerings. The idea of licensing (selling your name for others to place on their products) was still just a gleam in some marketing man's eye. So even though there were pedal cars that carried the names Pierce-Arrow, Packard, Buick, or Dodge, most had no association with the real cars they represented other than their name and some basic styling.

Another type of automobile that provided pedal car manufacturers with styling inspiration was the race car. With rapid technological improvement, automobile performance reached amazing levels in a fairly short time. In 1909 at the Brooklands raceway in Eng-

land, the Daimler Lightning was clocked at 127 miles per hour, roughly five times faster than Henry Ford's first Model T. In America, competing in the Indianapolis 500 provided early automotive manufacturers with a dramatic way to market the performance and reliability of their cars. Pedal car manufacturers were quick to offer miniature race cars complete with numbers painted on the radiator or side of the hood.

Improvements in manufacturing helped fuel the boom in the auto industry, most notably the assembly line and mass production made famous by Henry Ford and his Model T. By 1913, a Model T could be built in just 93 minutes, compared to 12 1/2 hours when production began in 1908. In addition, the price of the Model T had dropped from $850 in 1908 to just $440 in 1913. Strangely enough, no pedal car manufacturer produced a Model T when the car was in its prime. It was not until the 1960s that the Garton Company offered its "Tin Lizzie" as a homage to Henry Ford's car for the common man.

Tricycles of this type were manufactured from the late 1800s to around 1920, came in three different sizes and were made by different companies, such as Gendron, Toledo, Fairy, and Kirk Latty. The one in the photo was from about 1907 and is referred to as the Victorian style tricycle or girl's tricycle. The value of this tricycle today is between $500 and $2,500.

A joyful Easter!

In the century's second decade the same manufacturing methods that helped boost automobile production were starting to be applied to pedal car manufacturing as well. As more and more companies offered pedal cars to the public, less expensive models were introduced. Metal bodies became commonplace, and new finishes allowed color and style to take on more importance than ever. On the more expensive models, the attention to detail was greater than ever before. Nickel plating gave bumpers the luster of silver, padded seats provided junior drivers with more comfort behind the wheel, and decorative elements such as license plates, gauges, and hood ornaments brought a sense of refinement to the pedal car that took it beyond the realm of children's toys and carried it closer to a finely detailed miniature that was as much a work of art as a plaything for children.

Early pedal car manufacturing efforts in the United States centered on companies that made wheeled products such as baby buggies, wheelchairs, and bicycles. Since these companies were already involved in what was commonly known as the "wheeled goods" business, it made perfect sense for them to add pedal cars to their product lines. While several managed to produce pedal cars, they were not the main focus of any manufacturing company in the early years of the twentieth century. Propulsion for these early pedal cars still centered on the chain drive mechanisms used in bicycles or pedal mechanisms with steel rods connected to the rear axle. There were also some other notable (or odd) examples, such as the "hand cart," which was powered by a lever mounted in front of the rider that was pumped back and forth. This design never proved to be as popular as the pedal drive, though it reappeared from time to time in the pedal car world.

The story of the Gendron Manufacturing Company shares many common elements with other early pedal car makers. French

Canadian Peter Gendron was both an innovator and entrepreneur, traits that were common to early pedal car manufacturers. After creating a process for manufacturing spoked wire wheels, Gendron started a wheeled goods company in North Toledo, Ohio, in 1872. While Gendron managed to stay in business for five years making wheeled goods such as baby carriages and velocipedes, the venture ultimately failed. Not one to give up easily, the young Gendron continued to produce wheels and carriages at his home, and in 1880 he again created his own company, Gendron Iron Wheel.

Shortly after opening his new plant, Gendron created a new process for manufacturing lighter, stronger, and less expensive wire wheels. It quickly put his company in the forefront of bicycle producers. The word *Iron* was dropped from the name, and the Gendron Wheel Company proved to be quite a success for Peter Gendron. By 1890 his firm produced a full line of wheeled children's toys, plus wicker furniture and bicycles sold under the brand name "Pioneer." It was quite common in this time for one company to produce a wide range of products, and Gendron was obviously no exception. Soon wheelchairs were added to the line. As time went on, Gendron continued to improve his offerings and distribution, and his business flourished.

Another famous name in pedal cars was founded in Wisconsin in 1879 when E. B. Garton bought a wheeled goods company. All types of wagons, velocipedes, and other wheeled items soon carried the Garton name around the country. When the success of early automobiles captured the public's attention, Garton added pedal cars to his manufacturing efforts. Though the company underwent many changes, the Garton Manufacturing Company was one of the best-known producers of pedal cars for many years to come.

Garton's offerings for 1917 were typical for these early years of pedal car production. In that year when America entered World War I, Garton produced pedal cars with names like Winton, Buick, Packard, Pierce-Arrow, and Pope. All these pedal cars had bodies that were constructed of hard wood and steel and rode on spoked wheels fitted with thin rubber tires. The wheels were larger on the rear of the car and smaller in the front. All were powered by pedal drive. A few, like the Winton and Buick, were finished in multicolored paint schemes, but most were offered in solid colors. The Packard and Pierce-Arrow are illustrated in the company's catalog with the famous automobile names painted on the radiator, an early indication that pedal car makers were working hard to get their cars identified with the real autos of the day.

Other interesting offerings from Garton included a pedal car that looked more like the early automotive designs, such as the curved dash Oldsmobile of 1901. This particular pedal car, with the name *Rocket* stenciled on its side, was powered by pedal drive and rode

A rare pedal locomotive, believed to be from the Lines Brothers of England. Its value today is $10,000+.

on solid steel wheels. Even at this early time, the Barney Oldfield Racer from Garton proved that Americans' love of speed has never wavered. Barney Oldfield was a famous racing driver of the day who drove for Henry Ford. The pedal car that bore his name was inspired by early race car designs, complete with a rear gas tank and rounded hood. The Barney Oldfield Racer rode on four equal-sized wheels with thin rubber tires. It was offered in two different versions, with the more extravagant of the two featuring better quality wheels and two spare tires mounted on the rear gas tank.

Hugh Hill's early efforts at manufacturing a children's riding toy led him to create the rather novel Irish Mail, which featured a hand cart-style propulsion lever. In Britain, a similar vehicle was known as the Empire Racer. Though rather ungainly in appearance and fairly awkward to operate, the Irish Mail proved to be quite popular. Hill's company, based in Anderson, Indiana, was known as Hill Standard, and it was a large maker of wire wheels. With its success in the wheel business, Hill Standard, like so many other wheel producers of this era, manufactured a full line of wheeled goods, including pedal cars.

Another early pedal car manufacturer with midwestern roots was the Sidway-Topliff Company. Charles Sidway set up shop in Elkhart, Indiana, and soon began making a wide variety of products, including baby carriages. His business prospered, and he added pedal cars to the company's offerings. Sidway enjoyed tremendous success early in life, but died in his 30s, well before he could fully enjoy the prosperity that he found in the wheeled goods business.

With its emphasis on bicycle production in the late 1800s and early 1900s, Toledo, Ohio, was home to many successful wheeled goods companies. Among the most successful of these early manufacturers was the Toledo Metal Wheel Company, which was founded by Frank Southard. Toledo got its start by making bicycle and velocipede wheels in the 1890s. Shortly thereafter, they began producing a full line of children's wheeled goods. As the popularity of the automobile grew, Toledo added pedal cars to its manufacturing efforts by 1901.

Among its offerings were the Toledo automobile, powered by chain drive, and the Toledo Tandem, a two-seater based on the horseless carriage design. Toledo also offered the rather elaborate Empire Express Locomotive, powered by pedal drive. It came complete with a bell, smokestack, and headlamp. Toledo Metal Wheel was very successful and created pedal cars for its Blue Streak and Super Quality lines for many years to come.

While America certainly had a number of pedal car producers that filled the growing demand for these innovative children's toys, they were not alone in their efforts.

In Europe, pedal cars were being produced commercially in large numbers by 1910. Toy catalogs of the period offered a wide range of pedal cars and accessories. G & L Lines of London was a leading English producer of this period. The family company offered design improvements like the use of ball bearings throughout to make the car easier to turn and to pedal. Lines also added a fully operational hand brake for safety and used a fixed front axle that allowed for parallel steering. Lines was also the first manufacturer to use wheels of equal size. These design improvements would be carried over on almost all pedal cars in the years to follow.

As the pedal car market continued to grow, Lines introduced mass production manufacturing methods, which made their pedal cars even more affordable. By 1915 even the more affordable models produced by the company offered wheels of the same size at all four corners and parallel front wheel steering.

A hand car from the Irish Mail Line, circa 1915. It would sell today between $300 and $1,000.

By 1919, the second generation of the Lines family entered the toy business when the three sons of Joseph Lines joined forces to form Lines Brothers Limited. The Lines Brothers manufactured pedal cars under one of the most famous names from the early days of pedal cars—TRI-ANG. For more than half a century, TRI-ANG produced a full line of pedal cars that included luxury models, economy models, and even race cars.

Another early European pedal car producer of note is Giordani of Italy. Like many early pedal car producers, Giordani was a company that made many types of wheeled goods, including wheel chairs, tricycles, and children's toys. With the introduction of their first pedal car in 1915, Giordani produced pedal cars for many years, including eye-catching models inspired by race cars. Later, in the 1950s, the company produced a distinctive bullet-nosed Studebaker, based on the Studebaker styling of 1950.

When World War I sent the industrialized countries into battle in Europe, the manufacturing might of the world was soon directed toward war production. In addition to the changes in manufacturing needs that stymied pedal car production, the war-time drive for metals also took its toll by scrapping pedal cars that had already been produced. This fact, along with the relatively small number of pedal cars produced before the 1920s, makes these early examples extremely rare, and their value in today's market reflects their relative scarcity.

While the war effort certainly took its toll on pedal car production from 1914 to 1918, there were great times ahead for the pedal car. The stage had been set for the continued success of the automobile, and the pedal car's popularity only increased as the automobile became even more a part of people's lives. After the war, some factories returned to pedal car production and new manufacturers added their offerings. In the economic boom that followed, companies were created to devote more of their manufacturing efforts to the toys; but the pedal car got its start when those early automobiles made their noisy, smoky entrance on the roads, and the toy makers of the day noticed.

This postcard, titled "A Breakdown," was printed in 1912. It is representative of the earliest toy vehicles that actually looked like pedal "cars."

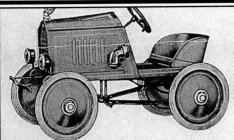

The premier line.... exactly modeled after real cars.... each with spring chassis .... lustrous enamel finishes in flashy color combinations .... black enameled gear ....black enameled steel front bumpers ..adjustable rubber pedals...metal headlights...nickeled motor-meter....gas lever. All except 1F833 have heavy steel crown fenders and aprons, and nickel trimmed wood running boards.

"VELIE"— Extreme length 35 in., Falcon tan enameled, blue & yellow trim and stripes, 10 in. red enameled double disc wheels, nickeled hub caps, ½ in. rubber tires.
EQUIPMENT—Cast steering wheel, imitation Klaxon horn.

1F833—1 in carton, 35 lbs.................................Each **$6.75**

"OAKLAND"— Extreme length 38 ½ in., Chrysler blue enameled, dark blue & yellow trim and stripes, 10 in. red enameled double disc wheels, nickeled hub caps, ½ in. rubber tires.
EQUIPMENT—Cast steering wheel, adjustable nickel trimmed windshield, license plate.

1F837—1 in carton, 45 lbs.................................Each **$9.25**

"MARMON"— Extreme length 41 ½ in., Drake blue enameled, tangerine & yellow trim and stripes, 10 in. tangerine **balloon type** double disc wheels, nickeled hub caps, 1 in. rubber tires.
EQUIPMENT—Composition steering wheel, adjustable nickel trimmed windshield, license plate, imitation Klaxon horn, realistic litho instrument board, gear shift.

1F840—1 in carton, 56 lbs.................................Each **$12.95**

"REO"— Extreme length 44 ½ in., Ottawa tan enameled, amber, red & yellow trim, 10 in. cream enameled heavy wire **auto type** wheels, enameled aluminum hub caps, 1¼ in. rubber tires.
EQUIPMENT—Cast steering wheel, adjustable nickel trimmed windshield, license plate, French (bulb) horn, realistic litho instrument board, gear shift, imitation leather cushion.

1F850—1 in wire bound box, 65 lbs.................................Each **$14.00**

"American-National" Aeroplanes

Double disc steel wheels (10 in. front, 7 in. rear), cast steering wheel with gas lever, 15 in. steel propeller with ratchet to produce motor sound.

"SPIRIT OF AMERICA"— Extreme length 44 in., wing spread 28 in., 5¾ in. steel wing, 1 in. wood fuselage, yellow enameled, red & black trim, green stenciled name, red wheels, ½ in. rubber tires.

1F881—1 in wire bound box, 31 lbs.................................Each **$6.75**

"AIR PILOT"— Extreme length 52 in., wing spread 30 in., 10¾ in. steel wing, shaped steel fuselage, tangerine enameled, sea green & yellow trim, yellow stenciled name, aluminum finish and black enameled 7-cylinder imitation motor, tangerine wheels, ⅝ in. rubber tires.

1F889—1 in carton, 45 lbs.................................Each **$8.50**

"AMERICAN-NATIONAL" DUMP TRUCKS

A sturdy line that is enjoying a tremendous popularity in a fast growing market. In this field it pays to sell the line children prefer....and that line bears the name "American-National".

Length 44 in., 10 in. red enameled double disc wheels, adjustable rubber pedals, black enameled cast steering wheel, gas lever, black enameled steel gear, black enameled steel front bumper, nickeled hub caps, license plate, imitation Klaxon horn. Each has large black enameled steel dump (raised and lowered by steel lever). End gate opens and closes automatically.

"JUNIOR"— Red enameled body, yellow trim, ½ in. rubber tires.   **$8.25**

"SPEED"— Larchmont blue enameled body, red & yellow trim, 1 in. rubber tires, heavy steel crown front fenders, oil can.   Each **$10.50**

Chapter Two

THE 1920s: MORE DETAIL AND SOPHISTICATION

After World War I, pedal car production took a significant turn for the better in terms of both quality and the variety of pedal cars—not to mention trucks and airplanes—produced. With the emergence of the automobile as a staple of American life, it was clear that fascination with the car would not end any time soon. As the economy of the 1920s began to roar, more and more people found the means to buy luxury goods for themselves and their children. Pedal car manufacturers scrambled to offer the buying public more choices, with a continued emphasis on creating detailed replicas of the real cars of the day. A 1925 pedal car advertisement

promised parents that they could buy their children "an automobile just like daddy's."

There were pedal car versions of automotive names that are still offered today, such as Chevrolet, Ford, Dodge, and Buick. There were pedal cars that sported names that have faded into the past: Reo, Oakland, Jordan, and Marmon. There were exquisitely crafted pedal car versions of the finest cars of the day, such as Cadillac, Packard, and Rolls Royce. Some of these luxury pedal cars offered fantastic amounts of detail, quality materials, and construction that far surpass today's standards of children's toys.

Pedal cars, which by this time were often advertised as

The Garton Toy Company began making children's wheeled toys in 1887. Despite two business-threatening fires, production continued and grew steadily, halting only for World War II. The company finally closed its doors in 1976.

This wonderful all-color advertisement for the American National Co. from an original catalog showing the premier line of the 1920s.

"juvenile autos," were an established segment of the toy industry. More manufacturers, including some who did not have the background in wheeled goods that the early manufacturers did, joined the ranks of pedal car makers to meet the growing demand. As is so often the case, the pedal car's growth and development followed that of the auto industry itself. The gains in popularity that pedal cars enjoyed in the 1920s can be linked in large part to the success that real automobiles had achieved by this time.

For everyday America, cars became more affordable and practical. The mass production methods made famous by Henry Ford and his Model T had become commonplace. Reliable, affordable transportation was more available than ever. Large auto makers like Ford and Chevrolet, which William C. Durant, founded with the Chevrolet brothers and then merged into the auto-making giant, General Motors (GM), built industrial empires by offering quality, mass-produced automobiles to the buying public. And the people bought them in record numbers. More than 4 million cars were produced in the United States in 1928.

While cars were becoming more plentiful and more affordable, they were also becoming

much more practical. The closed car quickly grew in popularity, so driving became a legitimate means of transportation year round. By the end of the decade, hard tops, or sedans, accounted for most of the production in the auto industry, and they cost little or no more than open-top automobiles. The electric light was improved and added to make nighttime driving a legitimate option, as opposed to the daredevil stunt that it had been with early oil or acetylene lamps. Electric starters, which first were offered along with electric lights on the 1912 Cadillac, became common, if not essential. It seems the buying public understandably had no desire to crank their car to life each morning, happy to avoid the danger this posed to life and limb.

Engines became more powerful, more reliable, and more well-mannered, giving drivers the power they craved without shaking them senseless. The tried-and-true four-cylinder engine powered most affordable cars, and did so better than ever before with improvements in valve and cylinder head design, increasing power substantially over the early four-bangers. For more upscale automotive offerings the new in-line, or "straight six," cylinder engines promised more power with less vibration and noise. They were available, at a rather substantial price increase, in cars from Buick, Chrysler, Chevrolet, and other manufacturers that wanted to offer a car a step above the basic transportation of the Model T.

At the head of the class, in terms of both performance and price, were the 8- and 12-cylinder engines. Certainly among the finest of these was the smooth-running Cadillac V-8, which offered a dual harmonically balanced

A 1922 model from The Diener Line by the American National Company of Toledo, Ohio. These cars, like many others, came in a standard or deluxe model with different names such as Stutz, Reliance, Junior, Hornet, etc. Today it would bring between $800 and $5,000, depending on condition.

"Off for the Studio." Here's Jackie Coogan, famous child movie-star, driving his custom American National pedal car in front of his Los Angeles home.

crankshaft design in 1925. These engines were fantastic feats of engineering that delivered massive amounts of silky, smooth power compared to the more meager engines of the day. They also had price tags that made them unobtainable to all but the most wealthy, discriminating drivers.

As engine power increased, better braking systems quickly became adopted throughout the auto industry, so cars could stop almost as well as they moved. Even so, it wasn't until the mid-1920s, or slightly later, that four-wheel brakes became the industry standard. And hydraulic, or power brakes, as we know them today, were only starting to become available. Tire technology, too, made dramatic improvements. The balloon tire was far better equipped to manage the deplorable road conditions of the day, giving early drivers a far better ride and more time spent driving, as opposed to fixing wheels.

While the engineers certainly had done their jobs making dramatic improvements in almost every mechanical system in the car, it was the stylists whose work was most noticeable.

windshield, and added finishing touches to give their cars a more complete appearance, particularly on luxury models. More distinctive design touches were incorporated into exterior parts like grilles, headlights, taillights, and trim pieces to help establish brand identity. Interiors were finished with leather and fine fabrics, and the layout of gauges and controls became more practical and helped give automobiles a more refined appearance. New paint technology allowed for a much wider selection of colors to be offered. This was the time when luxury cars like Packard, Duesenberg, Rolls Royce, Hispano-Suiza, and others set new standards for styling with their graceful, elegant designs.

Affordability and reliability were enjoyed by most drivers, but the 1920s also saw the creation of decidedly upscale automobiles that achieved a level of styling and performance that have made them timeless masterpieces of the auto maker's art. Even open-air

Another great European photo from a toy store of the 1920s. Imagine what a find this would be today.

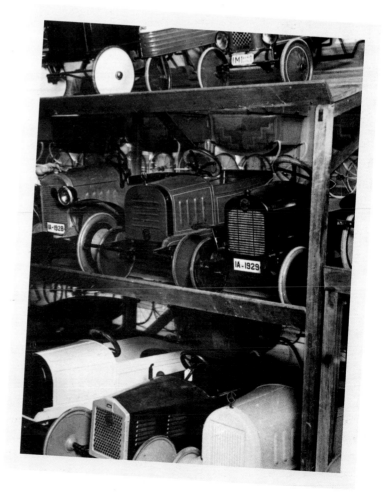

That, of course, was exactly as they intended it to be. Styling played a greater role in the auto industry as cars started to take on more individualized identities. Something was necessary in order to stand out from the crowd, since there were still literally dozens of auto manufacturers now offering their cars to the public. Many were assembled out of ready-made components, so the only real competitive edge that could be gained relied on the ability and imagination of the stylists and the people who marketed the car.

Auto manufacturers smoothed body and fender lines, raked the angle of the

This photo was taken in Germany during the 1920s. The sign in the upper right corner reads, "Please do not touch."

ACTUAL VISITS TO
P & G HOMES
No. 12

A little tinker gets just as smudged as a big one ~

We didn't see James Jr., right away. In the first place, he was almost invisible. And then, too, we were interested in our conversation with his mother—such a pretty, capable young person as she stood there on her trim front lawn, gardening trowel in hand.

We were talking to her about laundry soap just as we had talked to many other women in that small Ohio town.

"I've been using P and G for the last three years," she was telling us, "because if anyone needs a *good* laundry soap, I do. My small son gets his clothes so——"

And just *then* James Jr., appeared—from beneath a large yellow automobile we hadn't really noticed before. "Just look at me already, mother," he said apologetically. There on his nose was a great greasy smudge

—and on his white blouse, a much bigger, greasier smudge.

"Now you see why I use P and G," said his mother. "Thank goodness, dirt does come out with less trouble with P and G. I'll rub a little soap on that blouse and soak it tonight and by morning it will be practically clean. His colored blouses I just rub out with P and G and lukewarm water and they come out nice and fresh—with almost no rubbing too. P and G *is* such a good soap I never can understand why it costs so little."

Probably you, like James Jr.'s mother, have wondered why you actually pay *less* for this fine white laundry soap than you pay for even ordinary soaps of the same size and weight!

The reason really is: P and G's nation-wide

popularity. So many millions of cakes of P and G are sold every month all over America that Procter & Gamble, its makers, buy its fine materials in enormous quantities at great advantage. And they manufacture this fine soap at a smaller cost for a much larger cake than if they made less of it.

If P and G were *not* the largest-selling soap in the world, it would have to cost you much more than it does.

It is the largest-selling soap because it is such a *fine* soap. PROCTER & GAMBLE

FREE: *Rescuing Precious Hours*—"How to take out 15 common stains—get clothes clean in lukewarm water—lighten washday labor." Problems like these, together with newest laundry methods, are discussed in a free booklet—*Rescuing Precious Hours.* Send a post card to Winifred S. Carter (Dept. N Y 3), Box 1801, Cincinnati, O.

P AND G
THE WHITE
NAPHTHA SOAP

The largest-selling soap in the world

©1931, P. & G. Co.

motoring was reborn as the roadster found its way onto the scene. The top down, sleek styling of the roadster (usually backed up with plenty of power under the hood) made these two-seaters stylish transportation for those who could afford it. In an effort to make the roadster more practical, many were offered with an optional rumble seat that folded neatly into the trunk, keeping the beautiful, sporty lines of the roadster intact until the need for an extra seat arose. Originally, open-top cars were the least expensive models offered, but as closed cars became more popular, their prices dropped considerably. The sporty roadsters of the late 1920s, with their stylish good looks and details like fine wire wheels, were a way to offer the public an open-top car at an increased price.

Pedal cars eagerly followed all of these trends in the auto industry. Highly detailed models were available for buyers who had the means to pay for such luxuries. These finely crafted miniatures were by no means inexpensive. They had fine detailing that included simulated spark and gas controls on the steering wheel, gearshifts, cowl lights, and more. They were accessorized with toolboxes, spare tires mounted on the front fender, and even luggage racks.

For example, American National, which got its start in the 1920s when several pedal car manufacturers came together under a holding company, produced a fine Reo. Advertised in a 1920s catalog from Butler Brothers Distributors of New York, it cost $14 wholesale, while a real 1925 Chevrolet series K roadster, their most affordable model, sold for just $495. The pedal Reo was a large, well-built pedal car that measured 44 1/2 inches from bumper to bumper. It featured a spring chassis, wire wheels, and a heavy steel body finished in "Ottawa Tan enamel with amber, red and yellow trim." It rode on 1 1/4-inch rubber tires and was powered by pedal drive with adjustable pedals. It had wooden running boards, an adjustable windshield, and a hood ornament, all of which were trimmed in nickel. It was finished with a license plate, French bulb horn, gearshift, imitation leather seat cushion, and detailed instrument panel.

A 1924 Toledo advertisement for the company's "Super Quality Juvenile Automobiles" meticulously points out the impressive features of the "Deluxe" model, which rode on ball bearing disc wheels attached to a leaf spring chassis smoothed by ball bearing brackets. The Deluxe lived up to its name nicely, with hinged doors, a fully detailed dash, and a three-piece adjustable windshield complete with spotlight and windshield wiper. It sported a fender mirror, headlights with "nonglare lens," and rear stop signals for the ultimate in pedal car safety. Detailing was impressive to say the least, with a four-speed shifter complete with emergency brake, spare

tire mounted to the body on the driver's side, and a leather convertible top.

Manufacturing also became more efficient than ever, making basic pedal car designs more affordable to the average consumer. American National's Vellie cost just $6.75 wholesale, which was less than half the price of the finely detailed Reo. Although the Vellie didn't have fenders, running boards, or a windshield, it was still built of heavy-gauge steel and weighed 35 pounds. Finished in tan enamel trimmed in yellow and blue, the Vellie rode on 1/2-inch rubber tires mounted on 10-inch double disc steel wheels finished in red enamel and accented with nickel hubcaps. It

These bikes, velocipedes, and pedal cars are all from the Gendron line. The bikes were called the Pioneer Sidewalk Cycles. This photo was taken around 1928.

was typical of these work-based toys. The Speed was powered by pedal drive and rode on 1-inch rubber tires mounted on 10-inch steel disc wheels. It had a steel bed that could be raised and lowered by way of a lever mounted on the driver's side of the body. The end gate was hinged and would open automatically when the bed was raised. With its steel front fenders and wooden running boards trimmed in nickel, the Speed was finished in blue enamel with red-and-yellow trim. For added realism, it featured a klaxon horn, cast steering wheel, gas lever, and nickel-plated license plate frame and hubcaps. All this was available for a wholesale price of $10.50 from the Butler Brothers Distributors catalog.

The popularity of children's pedal-powered toys certainly got its start with the automobile, but these juvenile autos became so popular that manufacturers were quick to fill their line-ups with vehicles of every kind. Nothing was more technologically advanced in the 1920s than the airplane. The breakthroughs in aviation design gained during World War I took the airplane from a technological wonder to a common site at large public gatherings like fairs and festivals. Barnstormers thrilled audiences across the country with their acrobatic flying and daredevil stunts.

Always willing to take advantage of a trend, pedal car manufacturers soon included pedal-powered planes in their product lines. The American National Air Pilot was a large, 52-inch-long, finely constructed example of the pedal plane. It was orange with yellow-and-green trim and featured the Air Pilot name lettered on the fuselage near the tail. The Air Pilot had an imitation air-cooled radial engine and rode on 5/8-inch rubber tires mounted on steel disc wheels, which measured 10 inches tall for the pair of front wheels and 7 inches tall for the single tail wheel. The propeller was 15 inches long, constructed of

had a cast steering wheel, imitation klaxon horn, metal headlights, steel bumpers front and rear finished in black enamel, and, of course, it too sported a hood ornament, or "motormeter" as they were known at the time.

For children who wanted a more constructive pedal-powered vehicle, trucks were offered by several manufacturers. Fire trucks, complete with ladders, bells, and spotlights were introduced in the 1920s, and construction-inspired dump trucks gave children their own versions of the work vehicles of the day. The American National Speed dump truck

A 1928 Overland Whippet from the Pioneer line by Gendron. The pressed steel radiator shell was nickel plated. The instrument dashboard, flip-out windshield, a gear shift, and a really neat whippet dog hood ornament made this car extra special. Its restored value today is around $5,000.

steel, and featured a ratcheting sound-making device to give junior pilots as much realism as possible. This fine pedal plane sold for a wholesale price of $8.50 in Butler Brothers.

As pedal cars became a more established segment of the toy industry, larger manufacturers began to emerge. With its large number of bicycle factories and wheeled goods manufacturers, Toledo, Ohio, was called the "Coventry of the America"—a reference to the famous bicycle works in Coventry, England. While the comparison was accurate, by the end of the 1920s a better description for Toledo's manufacturing facilities would be that the city had become the Detroit of the pedal car world.

The American National Company was formed in Toledo when several smaller wheeled goods companies merged in 1925, in much the same fashion that General Motors was created during the previous decade. American National was the holding company that controlled Toledo Metal Wheel, National Wheel, and American Wheel. In 1927, Gendron Wheel joined American National as well. Pedal cars under the names American National, Toledo, and Gendron were pro-

duced at the Gendron plant, which covered nearly one square block of downtown Toledo.

Just like GM, which offered several auto marques, American National sold distinct lines of pedal cars, including Gendron's Pioneer and Skippy brands, American National's Sportster marque, and Toledo's Blue Streak and Super Quality lines. Skippy was a child's cartoon of the day that licensed its name to manufacturers of all types of children's toys— a forerunner of the common practice today.

American National produced a wide range of pedal cars, including fine offerings styled after Cadillac and Packard, with the latter being offered in both coupe and sedan designs. There were also Paiges, Reos, Hupmobiles, Oaklands, Marmons, and other makes that didn't survive as the auto industry grew and changed. Other models had names that are still common today, like Buick and Dodge. Vehicles, including stake body trucks, dump trucks, and fire trucks were also offered so children could have their own pedal-powered versions of everything from sporty roadsters to rugged, practical trucks.

continued on page 29

Following spread: Scott Weirick, Eric Folmer, and Courtney Wright are enjoying a nice summer picnic. This completely restored 1924 Chrysler by the Toledo of Ohio Co. would bring $8,000 or more.

25

Harold Chipman Jr. was five years old in 1928 when he was one of the lucky children receiving this American National pedal airplane for Christmas. Its restored value is more than $2,000.

Continued from page 25

Toledo offered a wide variety of pedal cars, including a popular hook and ladder fire truck, a fire chief's car, and cars styled from Willys-Knight, Jordan, Packard, Pierce-Arrow, Chrysler, and Hudson—even a Packard stake bed truck. These were well-detailed, finely constructed toys that had finishing touches like step plates on the running boards, folding luggage carriers mounted above the running boards, and actual die-cut vents on the hoods. They were built of heavy gauge steel, with a shipping weight of 110 pounds for the well-appointed Willys-Knight and a whopping 130 pounds for the hook and ladder truck!

The 1924 Toledo catalog listed more than two dozen models, among them an enclosed Cadillac coupe with tilt steering wheel, battery-operated lights, motor noisemaker, and hinged two-piece windshield. The Rolls Royce Victoria from the same catalog was a double phaeton design that had a rear seat, allowing it to carry a driver and a passenger. The Victoria also had a pair of windshields and was powered by a double pedal drive, so both riders could propel this 125-pound toy. It came finished with an on-board toolbox, spotlight, tilt steering wheel, and interior details like simulated gas and spark controls, a horn, and gearshift.

For the more sporty-minded kid, the Special Six race car successfully copied the "boat-tail" design of the day's racing machines. It also sported the long exhaust pipe that exited out the side of the hood and ran the length of the body, which was typical of racing cars of the 1920s. The Special Six racer rode on solid disc wheels and was powered

A 1928 American National Packard. Mention the names Packard and American National and both mean quality. The color, style, and finish of the real car are reflected in this model, making it very distinctive and desirable. Today's market value in restored condition would be more than $10,000.

It's 1925, and little Mary Virginia Johnson's father is gassing up her car in front of his store in Chuckatuoh, Virginia. The pedal car looks like it's from the Toledo of Ohio Co. line. Today this car would bring in excess of $5,000.

by pedal drive. For the ultimate in true automotive mechanical detail, the Haynes by Toledo featured a radiator that could be filled with water and drained by way of a valve at the bottom of the radiator.

Gendron, the last of the companies to be incorporated into American National was also offering a popular hook and ladder fire truck, a race car, a Jordan, a dump truck, and many more. Gendron was still touting the accomplishments of its founder, Peter Gendron, in its catalogs, with its Pioneer line—a reference to Gendron's early innovations and success in the wheeled goods business.

A 1928 Gendron advertisement touted the company's all-new Spirit of St. Louis plane, fully detailed to match its namesake. The Spirit of the St. Louis featured a Silver Bronze finish for added realism. Constructed

of metal, except for the propeller and rudder, the catalog promised that this pedal plane was an "exact duplicate" of the original that would do "everything but fly." With its balloon tires and solid disc wheels, the Spirit of St. Louis was available with pedal drive or with gear drive. Gendron also used the name, which they copyrighted, on a cheaper plane built of wood. It did not offer the detailing of the two metal models.

As far as automobiles went, Gendron was trying hard to convince the public that its pedal cars were as close to the real thing as possible. The catalog promised that the 1928 models came with "all the latest accessories" complete in the most popular colors of the day. Gendron pedal cars were "designed after the latest models in the automotive field." Their offerings included the typical cars

This 1920s fire truck is English made, believed to be from the Lines Brothers or TRI-ANG. Its value in restored condition is $6,000 to $8,500.

This 1929
Steelcraft 2.5-ton
Mack Junior
dump truck was
originally sold for
$14.98. Its value
in restored
condition is more
than $3,000.

(roadsters and speedsters), several fire trucks, a fire chief's car, dump trucks, and a toy boat.

At least one pedal car manufacturer who began production in the 1920s can trace its roots to the real automobile industry. Murray Ohio was founded in Cleveland and produced body parts for several car makers, including Chevrolet. Looking for a way to expand its business and diversify its product line, Murray started producing pedal cars under the name Steelcraft. By 1925, Steelcraft was offering almost a dozen different pedal cars, including a Packard Eight, Jordan Playboy, Chrysler Roadster, Overland Redbird, Buick Six, Cleveland Six, Jewett Roadster, Durant Special, Stutz Racer, Star Four, and Rickenbacker Flyer. Other offerings from later years included a Stutz, a Buick, and even a Mack truck. Later, tricycles and bicycles were added to the Murray line. While Murray struggled in the auto parts business, it found success with pedal cars and bicycles for many years to come.

The Garton Wheel Company from Wisconsin was another firm that produced a wide range of pedal cars, including models styled after Buick and Pontiac, a fire chief's car, and many more. For whatever reason, Garton often did not include the names of the real automobiles that its cars were styled after in the catalogs. Still, Garton offered more than a dozen models for 1927 and sold them under the Badger Line name, in honor of Wisconsin's animal mascot.

In Europe, pedal car production reached new heights of luxury and sophistication in the 1920s. For hundreds of years it had been common practice for craftsmen to create amazingly detailed, highly complex toys that were presented to the children of royalty and the upper class. As pedal cars became popular, this tradition helped to create fantastic examples of the toy cars that were far more technically advanced than anything offered to the buying public. The famous French auto maker, Andre Citroen, crafted miniature versions of some of his finest full-sized cars for a small, exclusive clientele.

Pedal cars experienced a phenomenal period of growth in the decade following World War I. The public embraced the idea of children's toys emulating the popular cars of the

This photo from the 1920s shows Johnnie W. Warner Jr. from Oneida, Tennessee, standing next to his beautiful American National Packard. If Johnnie owned this car today in excellent original condition it would bring over $10,000.

34

Original advertisements for pedal cars, such as this 1925 Steelcraft ad, are themselves very collectible and will demand top dollar.

day, and pedal car makers were able to supply them with more and better offerings. The emphasis on producing realistic toy versions of production cars made each company employ state-of-the-art manufacturing methods. At the same time, prices were kept in check and, in some cases, even lowered. But in October 1929, the stock market crashed and the economy reeled. Pedal car manufacturers found themselves struggling in the wake of the Great Depression, but pedal cars had established themselves as a popular segment of the toy industry. Not only did pedal cars survive, they thrived in these trying economic times.

Chapter Three

THE 1930s: DETROIT'S STYLING CHANGES ARE COPIED

The stock market crash of 1929 and the subsequent economic crisis that it helped spur, ushered in the 1930s on a rather ominous note. Indeed, the decade ahead was difficult for many pedal car manufacturers, and some did not survive. While pedal car prices were reduced and a number of lower-priced pedal cars were offered, pedal cars were still toys for the more well-to-do members of society.

At the same time, those who could purchase these toys for their children had a fantastic array of new products to choose from. During this decade, automotive styling experienced dramatic changes, and it was still critical for pedal car manufacturers to base their

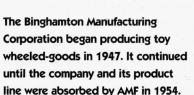

The Binghamton Manufacturing Corporation began producing toy wheeled-goods in 1947. It continued until the company and its product line were absorbed by AMF in 1954.

designs on the real cars of the day if they wanted to stay in the good graces of the buying public. As new automotive styles were introduced, pedal car manufacturers were quick to follow their lead. Since many of these new styles were noticeably different from previous designs, completely new models had to be developed and introduced. This was just one more example of pedal cars continuing to follow in the tire tracks of their full-sized counterparts.

Automotive styling in the 1930s found its inspiration by taking the automobile and creating a more complete package. The emphasis on incorporating the various parts of the car—grille, fenders, hood, windshield, roof, headlights,

One man's junk is truly another man's treasure. A few of the cars in this photo are: A 1933 Lincoln Speedster by American National, a 1940 Pioneer Roadster by Gendron, a 1951 Studebaker by Giordani, a 1932 Pontiac by Gendron, a 1934 Pontiac by Garton, and a 1935 Steelcraft.

This is a 1932 Essex Speedster by Steelcraft. It also came as a deluxe model with or without fenders, and in other colors.

Steelcraft also made a Mack hook and ladder truck in the 1930s.

and taillights into a more cohesive design were slowly taking hold by the early 1930s, but the trend was taken much further by automotive designers, accelerating as the decade went on. After these new styles became established with the buying public, there was no turning back for automotive design. Certainly the airplane had a hand in helping guide automotive stylists to a more streamlined or aerodynamic look; streamlining seemed to be everywhere by the late 1930s.

Taken to the extreme, streamlining could produce a rather ungainly look that left the public craving for more form and less function. This was certainly the case with the

THE LINE THAT *Gendron* SETS THE PACE

Pioneer Automobiles

No. 3610—Buick

Body—Length of rails 32-inches. Length overall 35-inches. Width at pedals 12-inches.

Finish—Body, hood and seat Jade green, striped and decorated in white. Wheels green, striped in white.

Equipment—As shown.

Wheels—9½ x ⅝-inch rubber tire disc.

Weight—34 lbs. Packed K. D. one in a carton.

No. 3611—Pontiac

Body—Length of rails 28-inches. Length overall 37-inches. Width at pedals 11-inches.

Finish—Body, hood and seat red, striped in white. Windshield red. Wheels red, striped in white. Aluminum front.

Equipment—As shown, including electric head lights.

Wheels—9½ x ¾ inch rubber tire artillery type.

Weight—38 lbs. Packed K. D., one in a carton.

No. 3612—Hudson

Body—Length of rails 28-inches. Length overall 41-inches. Width at pedals 11-inches.

Finish—Body, hood and seat yellow, striped in green and decorated in red. Windshield yellow. Front fender and running boards, red. Rear fenders, yellow. Wheels red, striped in green, decorated in yellow.

Equipment—As shown.

Wheels—9½ x ½-inch rubber tire disc.

Weight—40 lbs. Packed K. D., one in a carton.

Chrysler Airflow, introduced in 1934. Though it was an engineering triumph that featured early unibody construction, an automatic transmission with electronic overdrive, and an interior layout that produced a far better ride than other cars of the same era, the Airflow's radical styling was just too much of a good (engineering) thing. The Airflow's styling was based on early wind tunnel testing and not public opinion. As a result, the car performed well, but sales suffered quite a bit. DeSoto, launched by Chrysler as a slightly upscale companion brand in 1928, was stuck trying to sell nothing but Airflows for 1934. It proved to be

Gendron manufactured the Airflow under the trade names of American National, Skippy, and Toledo in 1934 and 1935. The Airflow had fine detail and style, and even included working headlights.

A 1930's European custom-made pedal race car. Estimated value—if found—would be $15,000+.

a tough year, with sales off by about 50 percent compared to 1933. The Airflow was offered in different forms by Chrysler until 1937, when it was discontinued.

Though the car was a commercial failure in the automotive world, Airflow pedal cars were offered by both Gendron and Steelcraft. The pedal-powered Airflows didn't seem to suffer the same fate as the car on which they were based. They bore an unmistakable resemblance to their namesake, and production continued until 1941. It seems that the looks of the Airflow didn't bother junior drivers, or their parents, when it came time to purchase a pedal car. They were offered in both Chrysler and DeSoto trim styles, and a dump truck and fire truck versions were also produced—two things that never saw the light of day as production vehicles.

While there was certainly an emphasis on styling, an automotive power struggle also took place in the 1930s. It was every bit as wild

as the horsepower wars that would take place in the 1960s, and it started on two separate fronts. One was the quest for power for the people in the form of inexpensive eight-cylinder engines. The other was launched by the luxury car makers, which tried to capture the public's attention by creating huge multicylinder engines that really upped the power ante.

Henry Ford's Model A was a serviceable car, and it sold quite well, with more than 1 million being produced for 1930. As the new decade dawned, however, times were changing and the Model A, with its four-cylinder engine, was lacking in horsepower, not to mention styling. Rival car makers, though still trying to compete with Ford on the low-priced front, touted their sleeker, more powerful six-cylinder cars as engineering triumphs. The Chevrolet six was a reliable, smooth, in-line engine that was well beyond the four-cylinder Ford in engineering sophistication and performance. And luxury car makers had taken their engines all the way to 16 cylinders, which put a little four cylinder to complete shame.

But in 1932, Henry Ford launched a surprise attack, in the form of his Model B, powered by the first inexpensive V-8, commonly known as the flathead. While other manufacturers had offered V-8s—Cadillac as early as 1915—Ford's V-8 was a powerful, refined motor for the masses. The flathead was the first affordable V-8 engine, and it helped changed everything automotive. Four cylinders were soon on their way out of favor, six cylinders became only adequate, eight cylinders were available to the

average working person, and luxury car makers continued to bring out the heavy artillery.

On the luxury car front, Cadillac was a major contributor to this cylinder battle. In its fight with Packard, Cadillac was looking for a knockout punch, something that would make big news with the car-buying public. Even those who couldn't afford a Cadillac (and they were many in the 1930s) would know that the company stood at the pinnacle of engineering and performance. So in December 1929, Cadillac came out with a V-16 engine, which put the Packard V-12 in a solid second place. It became clear that if you were a luxury car maker, you better have something more than a V-8 to get the public's attention.

This fascination with giant, expensive engines could not have come at a worse time in American history since the Great Depression was in full swing. Maybe it was some form of escapism for car buyers to imagine being able to afford one of these long and powerful V-12 or V-16 creations. Whatever the case, the public at large was enthralled with the V-16 Cadillac, and

MURRAY-OHIO SHOWS NEW CHRYSLER AIR-FLOW

Among the many new and interesting items shown in the 1935 catalog of the Murray-Ohio Mfg. Co. is the Chrysler Airflow No. 580 which is built for children from 3 to 8 years old. The hood is designed to resemble in detail the hood of the regular 1935 Chrysler Airflow automobile. The fenders are an integral part of the body, thus eliminating a large part of set-up costs and any possibility of the fenders becoming loose. The body is large and roomy, the car being easy running and built of 20 gauge automobile body steel. This car is equipped with electric headlamps.

Produced from 1935 to 1941, the Chrysler Airflow was sold under the Steelcraft name by Murray of Ohio. This model had working headlights, a French bulb horn, chrome bumpers, a windshield, and hood ornament. The most popular model was the maroon with ivory trim. Other models included the fire truck and dump truck. A nice original or restored Airflow today would bring more than $4,000.

A 1933 Plymouth by Steelcraft. This model was made for a few years with many different variations. Sometimes it was called a Nash, an Essex, or a Chevrolet, and seen in other colors.

it helped establish GM's top marque as the epitome of the American luxury car. While the really big motors were produced in rather small numbers for nearly a decade, the V-8 became the standard engine for most cars.

This cylinder race had an effect on styling as well. The hood had to grow quite a bit to make these monster motors fit in the car. The resulting long hood look, complete with louvers to allow for better cooling, was found on the most expensive cars and was completely functional. The manufacturers who created these behemoths had no choice but to stretch the hood to get all those cylinders to fit. Because these luxury cars were the automotive leaders of their day, it didn't take much time for the long hood look to catch on with other manufacturers. Long hoods were the required style whether the extra room under the hood was needed or not—and most cars certainly did not. This was one of the first examples of functionality turning into style, and the long hood can be seen on pedal cars like American National's early 1930s Packard roadster, which came complete with rumble seat and louvered hood.

Another couple of extremely rare Gendron products. Gendron designed and manufactured a great variety of pedal cars, hand cars, planes, racers, and much more. They were then sold under the trade names of Pioneer, Skippy, Express, Air King, Hi Speed, American, Toledo Blue Streak, American National, and others.

Phillips Tracy received this 1933 Buick by Steelcraft for his third birthday. This maroon and cream colored car has lots of character. It would sell for more than $8,000 in this condition today.

This 1936 Ford by Steelcraft was restored by co-author Ed Weirick with custom features such as the flip-out windshield, handmade banjo-style steering wheel, greyhound hood ornament, top boot, and original upholstery material. Its value today is more than $4,000.

For all the great engineering and styling triumphs of the decade, there was still a depression going on, and the ranks of auto manufacturing companies were reduced substantially by the end of the decade. The luxury car makers were especially hard hit. Auburn, Cord, and Duesenberg, which were all manufactured by the Cord Company of Indiana, were some of the finest automobiles ever built. They had amazing performance and innovative styling that was often imitated by other car makers; but for all their performance and innovation the company didn't make it past 1937, when Cord fell to tough times.

There were many other names that did not make it past the 1930s. Names such as Pierce-Arrow, Stutz, La Salle, Oakland, Marmon, and Jordan disappeared. In the wake of the Great Depression the nation was left with the big three: General Motors, Ford, and Chrysler. These companies had learned the lessons of automotive efficiency, and their new shape so overwhelmed the remaining manufacturers, such as Packard, Hudson, and Nash,

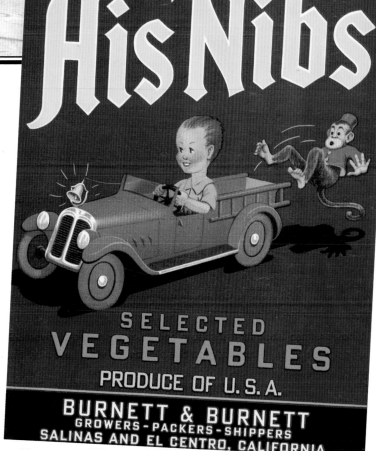

You never know where you'll find great ads with pedal cars! Ads of this type are highly collectible and sought after.

Pioneer Automobiles

No. 3666—Fire Captain

Body—Length of rails 28-inches. Length overall 41-inches. Width at pedals 11-inches.

Finish—Body, hood and seat red, striped in white. Fenders red. Wheels red, striped in white. Aluminum front.

Equipment—As shown.

Wheels—9½ x ½-inch rubber tire disc.

Weight—42 lbs. Packed K. D., one in a carton.

No. 3668—Fire Captain

Body—Length of rails 32-inches. Length overall 44-inches. Width at pedals 12-inches.

Finish—Body, hood and seat white, striped in green, decorated in red.

Equipment—As shown, including electric headlights.

Wheels—9½ x ⅝-inch rubber tire disc.

Weight—50 lbs. Packed K. D., one in a carton.

No. 3673—G-Man Cruiser

Body—Length of rails 32-inches. Length overall 44-inches. Width at pedals 12-inches.

Finish—Body, hood and seat white, striped and decorated in green and red. Fenders green. Wheels white, striped in green.

Equipment—As shown, including realistic G-MAN gun, manufactured by Louis Marx & Company.

Wheels—9½ x ⅝-inch rubber tire disc.

Weight—47 lbs. Packed K. D., one in a carton.

Page Forty-four

Gendron Wheel Company of Toledo, Ohio: One of the top names in "Juvenile Conveyances." The Gendron Company is still in business after 127 years.

that these "independents" would never again be really competitive.

Unfortunately for the pedal car, its manufacturers were also plagued by the effects of the tremendous economic downturn of the 1930s. Toys of any kind are luxury goods, and expensive toys even more so. Some of the largest manufacturers in the business suffered greatly, and few new names arrived to challenge them.

While they may have suffered during the 1930s in terms of sales, the pedal car manufacturers still created more elaborate and complete pedal cars than they had in the previous decade. Two-tone paint schemes, often found on upscale models, were more popular than ever. Battery-powered lights, horns, and motor hummers (which added engine sounds to the cars) were very popular by the mid-1930s. Chrome and aluminum took the place of nickel plating in an effort to reduce costs while still giving pedal car trim the chance to shine. The artillery wheel, which featured rather substantial steel spokes, found widespread acceptance in the ranks of pedal car manufacturers who outfitted many of their models with these sturdy, but stylish wheels. All these improvements, produced by pedal car manufacturers who were committed to building well-designed and well-built toys made the 1930s a fine decade for pedal cars, regardless of the trying economic conditions.

From its founding in 1925, American National had quickly grown to become the world's largest manufacturer of pedal cars. Under its own name, and the labels of Gendron and Toledo, American National produced pedal cars for a buying public that, for a time, couldn't seem to get enough of these wonderful toys. Unfortunately, the company's lack of diversification savaged its balance sheet as the nation reeled from the Depression. The company was restructured, but the results remained the same. Though they would continue to produce pedal cars until

Steelcraft produced this car from 1935 to 1937 as a Chevrolet. It has neat headlight pods and came with a windshield and hood ornament. The fire chief version came with a bell and no windshield.

World War II began, the 1930s were American National's last full decade of production.

To get a clear look at the scope and quality of pedal cars in the 1930s, consider the offerings of Gendron in 1936. As part of American National, Gendron offered a full line of pedal cars, trucks, and planes. But to get the most out of the money it spent on manufacturing capacity, some models were produced under the American National and Toledo names as well.

Each American National marque had divisions within itself. Gendron's Pioneer line offered a wide variety of pedal car styles that were designed to fit budgets that ran from moderate to extravagant. The 1936 Gendron catalog lists well-known names such as Chevrolet, Buick, and Dodge among the models sold. These cars were certainly the more affordable models, with a fenderless design and minimal trim. There were also Auburn and Pontiac models that, while fenderless, came with working headlights.

Upscale offerings had bodies that featured nicely rounded fenders, both front and rear, connected by running boards. They also sported two-toned paint schemes that added to their realism. There was a Hudson finished in yellow and red, a Pierce-Arrow in buff and tan, a Ford in green and cream, and an Oldsmobile in black and cream that came complete with working headlights. There was also a fine looking Auburn in red with pneumatic tires, working headlights, and a working horn.

Gendron also sold a pair of fire chief's cars, one finished in red and a more expensive version with a two-tone white-and-red paint scheme and working headlights. The G-Man Cruiser managed to combine the appeal of the pedal car with that of the toy machine gun. It was finished in cream and green, and the machine gun mounted on the hood was manufactured by the Marx Company.

There was also a pedal car based on a famous race car design of the 1930s. Finished in

A few more of Steelcraft's neat little cars from the 1937 catalog.

Chief Automobile
Model No. 515
(For Children 2 to 5 Years)

OVERALL DIMENSIONS: Length, 33½"; width, 16".
EQUIPMENT: Long type headlights (non-electric), Fire Chief bell, bracket, pull cord, transfers, etc.
WHEELS: 8¼" Double disc with ⅝" black rubber tires. Wheels are artillery type with large dome hub caps.
FINISH: Body in Red baked enamel with Ivory trim. Wheels in Ivory with Black stripe.
SHIPPED: One in a carton, K. D. WEIGHT: 27 lbs.

Automobile
Model No. 505
(For Children 2 to 5 Years)

OVERALL DIMENSIONS: Length, 33½"; width, 16".
WHEELS: 8¼" Double disc with ⅝" black rubber tires. Artillery type with large dome hub caps.
EQUIPMENT: Long type headlamps (non-electric) motometer.
FINISH: Body in Green, with Ivory trim. Wheels in Ivory.
SHIPPED: One in a carton. WEIGHT: 26 lbs.

This is the Ace Automobile by Steelcraft. This cute little Speedster model was made from 1937 through the 1940s and also came as a Fire Chief. Sitting at the wheel in 1941 is 2 1/2-year-old Bob Stump. In restored condition this pedal car would bring about $1,500.

Ace Auto
Model No. 500
(For Children 1½ to 4 Years)

SPECIFICATIONS

OVERALL DIMENSIONS: Length, 31¼"; width, 15½".
FINISH: Body in Red. Wheels in Ivory striped in Red. Undergear in Red. All in baked enamel.
WHEELS: 8¼" double steel disc with ½" rubber tires.
SHIPPED: One in a carton K. D. SHIPPING WEIGHT: 22 lbs.

white with a large red "99" painted on its nose, the Skippy racer had the aerodynamic pointed tail that so many early race cars featured. It rode on pneumatic tires with ball bearings and came complete with a detailed dash and a horn—to get the slower traffic out of the way.

By far the biggest, most detailed pedal car offerings from Gendron in 1936 were the fire trucks. There were two models of the Hose Cart available, both of which were finished in red with plenty of striping and came equipped with ladders and a real rubber hose with a brass nozzle. They both had electric headlights,

JUVENILE STEELCRAFT VEHICLES

FUNDAMENTALLY, as an arm exerciser for children, the speed car should be one of the most popular pieces of Juvenile Wheel goods. The Steelcraft Cars are built for speed. Every line of them conveys the idea of speed to the child. And furthermore, real speed can be developed on them with a minimum of effort by the child. No store should be without them.

Ball Bearing
Chain Driven

"Playboy" Speed Car
Chain Driven
Model No. 590

OVERALL DIMENSIONS: Length, 40"; width, 14½".
WHEELS: Front, 8" roller bearing. Rear wheels (2), 10" roller bearing with ¾" black rubber tires.
DRIVE: The mechanism propelling this speed car is chain driven type, no meshing or wearing of gears. Five ball bearings are used to reduce friction and add to speed.
FINISH: Red baked enamel, with Ivory trim.
PACKING: One to a carton. SHIPPING WEIGHT: 33 lbs.

Ball Bearing Direct Drive

"Playboy" Speed Car
Direct Drive
Model No. 591

OVERALL DIMENSIONS: Length, 32½"; width, 13½".
WHEELS: Front, 6"; rear wheels, 8" with ½" rubber tires.
DRIVE: The drive is direct from a cranked rear axle. Three ball bearings are used to minimize friction. This drive is speedy and cannot get out of order.
FINISH: Red with Ivory wheels.
PACKING: One to a carton. SHIPPING WEIGHT: 18 lbs.

GREATEST IN PLAY VALUES

spotlights, and a working fire bell. The larger of the two featured an electric horn and motor hummer. It weighed an incredible 120 pounds for shipping.

By 1938, Gendron also offered some interesting departures from the standard pedal car and truck designs. There was the Pioneer Locomotive, a great example of the streamline trains of the day. Finished in red and lettered with the words *City of Denver*, it was equipped with a bell under the cowl and a battery-operated headlight. Gendron also offered a trailer for its cars. This was the perfect way for a pedal car driver to bring a passenger along for the ride. The trailer was finished in silver and green and featured a window in front and a folding seat in the rear. It included a coupling kit so it could be towed by any pedal car.

The Gendron Skippy roadster had the forward-leaning look that was becoming popular with automotive designers during this time. The V grill and bullet headlights mounted on top of the front fenders were also design features

This 1937 catalog shows that Steelcraft made a great exerciser for kids. Its value today is in the neighborhood of $500.

A restored 1938 Ford Deluxe by Garton with Eric Folmer and Blair Pooler at play.

Another very desirable and sought-after car is this 1937 Dodge by Steelcraft. Like the Auburn Streamliner, it has headlight pods on the side of the body, and the windshield, front bumper, hubcaps, and artillery wheels are of a similar nature. Many models from each manufacturer had interchangeable parts to help keep the production cost to a minimum. *Zone Five*

A 1938 Pioneer Roadster by Gendron. Its overall length was 36 inches with artillery wheels. It came in several color combinations. Both front and rear fenders were an integral part of the body. This model is greatly sought after today.

This photo was taken in Maine during 1938. Pictured are Fred J. Brown, two years old, and brother Noel Brown, three years old in their Gendron Roadster. If this car were restored today it would bring $2,500 to $4,000.

CHRISTMAS TOYMAKERS TURN TO SCIENCE & INDUSTRY FOR NEW IDEAS

At the preview of new Christmas toys held in New York from Oct. 25 to Nov. 1, there was no trace of the stuffed rocking horses of the Age of Innocence or the fairy princesses of Grimm and Andersen. The industrial revolution has definitely caught up with the toy world. Supreme among the new toys are miniature replicas of streamlined automobiles and busses, spacious trailers, television radios and telephones, four-motored airplanes, WPA road construction sets, "functional" dolls that live in modern houses. For their inspiration, toy manufacturers now turn to the world of industry and science, the comic strip, the movies and radio. The sensation of the toy world this year is a $10 miniature of the saucy radio dummy, Charlie McCarthy.

About $230,000,000, the highest figure in seven years, will be spent by the U.S. public this year for toys, predicts James L. Fri, managing director for the Toy Manufacturers of the U.S. War toys, popular abroad, will account for less than 1 percent of the total. With American children, games based on crime-solving, business and sports outnumber military strategy 1,000 to 1. The American dolls wear party frocks and rompers. Foreign dolls wear uniforms.

Trailers of all sizes promise to be as popular in the toy world this year as they were in the adult automobile world last year. The trailer (*above*), big enough to ride in, is typical of a score of models available, costs $14.95.

that were common to full-sized automobiles of the late 1930s. The roadster was finished in two-tone red with cream-colored fenders on artillery wheels. It was also sold in blue and cream with solid disc wheels and pneumatic tires. Both models were equipped with electric lights and an electric horn.

Gendron's sister maker, American National, was certainly not lacking in quality or styling despite the tough economic times. American National's offerings during the 1930s were similar in selection and quality to Gendron, with some models being produced by both companies. There were pedal cars with famous automotive names such as Overland, Chevrolet, Buick, Auburn, Lincoln, La Salle, Cadillac, and Packard.

American National made dump trucks that took on the names of famous truck makers like

White. The company also offered finely crafted fire trucks that would delight any child. There were pedal-powered planes, including American National's own version of *The Spirit of St. Louis,* Charles Lindbergh's famous plane from his solo New York-to-Paris flight in 1924. The Wright Whirlwind, also by American National, was a tri-motor pedal version of the famous Wright aircraft design.

By the mid-1930s, many of American National's pedal cars were equipped with working headlights. The more detailed offerings also had battery-operated taillights, horns, and engine noisemakers. There were full balloon tires on some models, and the artillery wheel was popular.

Toledo produced pedal car versions of cars by Lincoln, Pontiac, Buick, Chrysler, Hudson, and Hupmobile in the early 1930s. There was

Another of the Gendron Company's Pioneer Roadsters with the rare Skippy trailer. The roadster is a deluxe model with an opening hood and imitation motor.

The Twentieth Century Limited

(The Child can ride and steer this Train Set)

THIS Train Set offers untold play value to the child. It is built entirely of 20 gauge automobile body steel. The child seated on the cab of Locomotive or Express Car can ride and steer it from the smoke stack or brake wheel. Coupling is provided to connect Express to Locomotive.

Model No. 286
Express Car De Luxe
Equipped with 2 electric lights—rear of car

OVERALL DIMENSIONS: Length 23¾", Width 6½", Height 10½".

WHEELS: Solid rubber wheels.

EQUIPMENT: Has coupling to attach to Locomotive, Sliding door, and steers from brake wheel.

FINISH: Body in brilliant Red baked enamel. Doors in White baked enamel. Wheels in White baked enamel.

PACKING: One in a certified shipping carton.

WEIGHT: 11 lbs.

Model No. 285
Locomotive De Luxe
Equipped with electric headlight

OVERALL DIMENSIONS: Length 28", Width 6¾", Height 10½".

WHEELS: Double steel discs with solid rubber tires.

EQUIPMENT: Bell and pull cord, and coupling to attach to Express Car. Steers from top of stack.

FINISH: Boiler, tender and frame in lustrous White hard baked enamel. Cab, catwalk, wheels, Red baked enamel. Hand rails nickel plated.

PACKING: One in a certified shipping carton.

WEIGHT: 13 lbs.

Can be purchased as complete set, or individual items, as desired.
(Batteries not included.)

Model No. 156 Express Car—without lights

LENGTH: 18". Steers from top. Child can ride on this item. Has steel wheels.

FINISH: Red body, Black wheels, Green door (Doors slide).

PACKED: Each in a carton.

SHIPPING WEIGHT: 8 lbs.

Model No. 155 Locomotive

Steers from top. Child can ride on cab

LENGTH: 22".

WHEELS: Heavy steel wheels.

FINISH: Red with Black cab.

PACKED: One in a carton.

SHIPPING WEIGHT: 9 lbs.

Page Fifty-one

This page from a 1937 catalog shows that Steelcraft made fine toys other than just pedal cars. Many of these today will bring top dollar.

also a fine Duesenberg Racer, along with models styled on Cords and Marmons. Toledo's "tandem" pedal car held a pair of riders and featured dual pedal drive. There were also hook and ladder trucks, hose cart fire trucks, and dump trucks well represented in Toledo's catalog. Several truck models carried names such as GMC and White, and many rode on pneumatic balloon tires mounted on wire wheels. Other pedal-powered craft produced by Toledo included a pedal boat, a pair of locomotives, and several pedal planes.

By the mid-1930s, Toledo offered Chrysler's radical Airflow design in both the Chrysler and DeSoto trim. There were a host of beautifully crafted pedal cars that came with electric lights, including models with names such as Auburn, Hudson, Nash, Buick, La Salle, Packard, Cord, and Cadillac. The Cord and Cadillac also featured electric taillights and a spare tire mounted on the running board. By 1936 there were newly styled cars modeled on Cadillacs and Lincolns, both of which had electric headlights and horns. The G-Man Cruiser was introduced, and the Airflow had electric headlights.

Murray Ohio, which produced the Steelcraft line, was certainly not to be outdone by American National. Keeping the competition intense, Murray managed to take pedal cars to a whole new level of styling and sophistication by associating with Count Alexis de Sakhnoffsky, who was a leading designer of the day. The Steelcraft catalog promised that its 1937 offerings were "the finest we have ever produced" while still trying to keep prices reasonable. They justified the expense of offering such fine pedal cars because "this year promises to be the biggest year in the sale of large automobiles, and we have found that when there is a large volume on large automobiles there is likewise a large volume of Juvenile Automobiles." Unfortunately, 1937 was the same year the Cord Company, which also produced Auburn and Duesenberg, went out of business. Murray's prediction on the car market may have been off, but its pedal cars were still terrific.

The Steelcraft cars for 1937 were headlined by the Super Charger, which shared both its name and styling with the Auburn 851 Super Charger. It was a gorgeous toy, *continued on page 57*

continued on page 57

This 1937 Steelcraft Chrysler Airflow is very rare in this Playboy Trucking Company model. All models were equipped with electric headlights and a Chrysler radiator ornament. The original price in 1937 was $9.85. Today in restored condition it would cost about $6,000.

A 1939 Lincoln Zephyr by Steelcraft and a 1968 Murray Jolly Roger Flag Ship boat on a trailer. The Lincoln Zephyr was linked to the real car of that time and had distinctive lines that have made it more desirable than ever today. It came in several color combinations and would sell for $4,000 today in restored condition. The Murray Jolly Roger, or any similar models, such as the Skipper or Dolphin, came in deluxe or standard models. The difference would be the addition of a windshield, rail, or outboard motor.

AUTOMOBILES

No. 500

Model No. 500

ACE AUTO
(For Children 1 to 3 Years)

Overall dimensions—Length 31¼"; width 15½". **Wheels**—New 8" beaded disc wheels with large beaded hub caps and ½" solid rubber tires. **Equipment**—Motometer. **Finish**—Body in Red with Ivory trim. Wheels Ivory with bright plated hub caps. **Packed**—One to a carton. **Weight**—21 lbs.

List Price $7.00

Model No. 525

FORD AUTOMOBILE
(For Children 2 to 5 Years)

Overall Dimensions—Length, 35½"; width, 16". **Wheels**—8¼" double disc with ⅝" black rubber tires. Artillery type, with large dome hub caps. **Equipment**—Motometer, windshield, bulb horn, new streamline lights (non-electric). **Fenders**—The fenders are an integral part of the body. **Finish**—Body in Maroon baked enamel, striping in Ivory. Wheels in Ivory. **Packed**—One to carton. **Weight**—30 lbs.

List Price $11.50

No. 525

No. 526

Model No. 526

FORD CHIEF AUTOMOBILE
(For Children 2 to 5 Years)

Overall Dimensions—Length, 35½"; width, 16". **Wheels**—8¼" double disc with ⅝" black rubber tires. Artillery type, with large dome hub caps. **Equipment**—Fire Chief bell, pull cord and transfers, new streamline lights (non-electric). **Fenders**—The fenders are an integral part of the body. **Finish**—Body in Red, with Ivory trim. Wheels in Red with Black stripe. **Packed**—One to carton. **Weight**—30 lbs.

List Price $11.50

A 1939 catalog page showing three very desirable pedal cars from the Steelcraft Co.: the Ace, and two models of the 1936 Ford. Any of these today in nice original condition would bring $2,500+.

From 1938 to 1941 this Oldsmobile was produced by Steelcraft. Like a few of the other Steelcraft cars of the same era (like the Buick, Dodge, Chrysler, and Lincoln Zephyr) all had a very recognizable style and are very much sought after by collectors today. Unfortunately, the hood ornament is wrong on this car, but it doesn't hurt the value too much. Today, in restored condition, it would fetch around $4,000. *Zone Five*

Continued from page 53

with the swept-back body lines of the Auburn. It featured exposed exhaust pipes, a double leaf front bumper and a highly raked windshield, all in chrome plate. It was finished in maroon enamel with ivory trim and rode on ball bearing artillery wheels. It also had a ball bearing spring chassis and was finished with a detailed instrument panel, padded seat, and French bulb horn. The Streamliner also featured the styling flair of the Count. It was finished in red, and the body, made of heavy gauge steel, had beautiful, sweeping lines that put it at the forefront of automotive toy design.

Steelcraft also offered its version of the Chrysler Airflow design, finished in maroon enamel and trimmed in ivory. It rode on artillery-style wheels and had nicely detailed Airflow headlights, a French bulb horn, and a Chrysler hood ornament.

An extremely rare pioneer locomotive from the Gendron Co. Line. Today an excellent original sells for $10,000+.

There was also a Ford, with streamlined headlights, a bulb horn, and skirted rear fenders, which had become so common. The Ford was offered in maroon with ivory trim, a color combination that proved to be very popular with Steelcraft in 1937. A fire chief's version of the Ford was also available. It was finished in red with ivory trim and came with a bell.

On a lower-priced level, Steelcraft offered fenderless pedal-powered cars, identified in the catalog rather unimaginatively as "automobile." It may have lacked fenders, but it did have the swept-back headlights that seemed to be so popular and came with a hood ornament as well. It rode on artillery wheels and was available in ivory or green and, as a fire chief's car, in red with the hood ornament replaced by a bell.

Steelcraft also offered several trucks, including models that imitated the 1- and 2-ton Mack dump trucks, both of which had pedal-drive,

artillery wheels, and were finished in red enamel. The 2-ton was the more refined of the pair. It came with fenders, running boards, a gearshift, and bulb horn. The catalog promised it was capable of carrying payloads of up to 150 pounds! The 1-ton was also available as a hook and ladder fire truck, complete with a bell. By far the most interesting truck offering from Steelcraft was its Airflow dump truck, which took the Airflow body style and added a work-ing dump bed behind the driver's seat. The Airflow's unique styling hardly seemed to lend itself to life as a dump truck, but that didn't stop Steelcraft from trying to get the most vehicles it could out of its existing body styles.

Garton Manufacturing was another company offering a wide range of pedal cars during the 1930s. It produced models based on styles from Chrysler, Pontiac, Reo, Cadillac, Packard, Nash, Buick, Oldsmobile, Ford, and Lincoln. Garton also offered pedal airplanes, including a U.S. mail plane and a Curtiss monoplane. There were several of the ever-popular fire trucks, including a hook and ladder and fire chief's car. There were also dump trucks that carried the names of famous truck makers such as Speedwagon and Diamond T. By the mid-1930s, several Garton models, including their version of the Lincoln Zephyr, as well as pedal cars styled after La Salle, Chevrolet, and Buick models, came with battery-powered headlights.

For all the fine pedal cars produced in the 1930s, there were pedal car manufacturers that could not survive, including Sidway Toppliff, which barely made it into the 1930s intact. Hill Standard also fell to the tough economic times and left the ranks of pedal car producers. Still, the 1930s proved to be a decade unmatched in pedal car selection and quality. Soon, however, things would change dramatically. By 1939 war raged in Europe, and pedal car makers had to turn their attention away from toys to the tools of war.

Chapter Four

THE 1940s:
THE WAR CHANGES
EVERYTHING

The 1940s was really a decade in three parts: the short time before World War II, the war years, and the giddy peace that followed. For pedal car manufacturers, things continued relatively unchanged before the war, but afterward the pedal car world became quite different. Worldwide conflict and a shift to all-out military production put a halt to pedal car manufacturing. Instead, each company turned its attention to making goods for the war effort. After the war, when pedal car production resumed, some of the biggest names in the business were

Founded in 1900, American Machine and Foundry grew to become one of the largest wheeled-goods manufacturers in the country. In 1982, the company's toy division was acquired by bicycle maker Roadmaster who continues to build bicycles and riding toys.

gone. New manufacturers came in to replace those that had left, but more was lost in the 1940s than these business changes had shown.

In terms of sophistication and style, the 1920s and 1930s set the high-water mark for pedal cars. It seemed that pedal car manufacturers were constantly trying to come up with the most innovative styling and the greatest amount of detail they could possibly offer. There were pedal cars with battery-powered headlights, horns, and even a few sound makers designed to create engine noise. There were flowing designs with

The driver of this deluxe Pontiac wagon with canopy by the Murray Company is Carl Plavan from Avon, Ohio. Murray made this model as a coupe, a fire chief car, a fire truck, and a wrecker from 1941 to 1950.

61

AUTOMOBILES

ZEPHYR DELUXE AUTO
No. A573
SPECIFICATIONS

Overall Dimensions—Length, 42½"; width, 17½".
Wheels—10" ball bearing with 2¾" white side-walled pneumatic tires.
Equipment—Complete—French bulb horn, adjustable rubber pedals, radiator ornament, seat pad, Swiss music box radio, windshield, bumper, hub caps and fender lights.
Finish—Body in Black baked enamel with Ivory panelling. Wheels in Black. Windshield, bumper, hub caps and fender lights all chromium plated.
Packed—One in a carton. **Shipping Weight**—45 lbs.
    Construction reduces dealer's set-up work to a minimum.

No. A573
(For Children 3 to 6 Years)

List Price..$31.16

ZEPHYR AUTO
No. A574
SPECIFICATIONS

Overall Dimensions—Length, 42½"; width, 17½".
Wheels—10" new style double disc, roller bearing with 1¾" white sidewall semi-pneumatic, puncture proof tires. New style hub caps.
Equipment—Headlamps, French bulb horn, front bumper, windshield, adjustable rubber pedals, radiator ornament, seat pad and steering wheel. Fenders are a part of body.
Finish—Body in two tone Blue baked enamel with White trim. Wheels in Red. Windshield, steering wheel, bumper and headlights chromium plated.
Packed—One in a carton. **Shipping Weight**—45 lbs.
    Construction reduces dealer's set-up work to a minimum.

List Price..$24.20

No. A574
With 1¾" white side-walled
puncture-proof tires
(For Children 3 to 6 Years)

CHRYSLER AIRFLOW
No. A580
SPECIFICATIONS

Overall Dimensions—Length, 43¾"; width, 18".
Wheels—10" Roller bearing, artillery type with ¾" rubber tires and large plated dome hub caps.
Equipment—Headlamps, French bulb horn, front bumper, windshield, ball bearing spring type chassis, adjustable rubber pedals, Chrysler radiator ornament and steering wheel. The fenders and running boards are a part of the body.
Finish—Body in Maroon baked enamel with Ivory trim. Wheels, steering wheel, bumper, windshield, headlights in Ivory.
Packing—One to carton. **Shipping Weight**—50 lbs.
    The construction of this Auto reduces set-up work to a minimum.

No. A580
(For Children 3 to 8 Years)

List Price..$18.48

TRACTOR
No. A690
SPECIFICATIONS

Overall Dimensions—Length, 43"; height, 26".
Wheels—Beaded rear 16" diameter with 1¼" solid rubber tires. Beaded front 8½" diameter, with ¾" solid rubber tires. Equipped with new plated hub caps.
Equipment—Adjustable rubber pedals, spring saddle, draw bar.
Finish—Body and wheels in Red baked enamel with Ivory trim. Seat and undergear in Black.
Packed—One in a carton. **Shipping Weight**—52 lbs.

List Price..$15.82

No. A690
(For Children 4 to 7 Years)

Check out these prices. These are all from the Steelcraft line from 1940.

graceful curves and bodies of heavy-gauge steel with nickel- or chrome-plated trim parts. It was an amazing time for pedal car manufacturers, but it did not last forever.

This is not to say that pedal cars of the early 1940s were somehow flawed or lacking in quality. These prewar toys were still well built; almost all were constructed with heavy-gauge steel and weighed between 35 and 70 pounds. They rode on ball bearing wheels for smoothness and ease of operation. Semipneumatic tires, complete with white walls, had been introduced and were quite popular. One of the most well-detailed pedal cars produced during this period was the great 1940 Gendron Pioneer Roadster. It had a working hood that could be raised to reveal a mock engine. There was nothing wrong with these pedal cars, but the economic realities of the Depression took their toll and many companies could not afford to produce the meticulously detailed, finely finished miniatures that they sold in the 1920s and 1930s.

It has been shown time and again how pedal cars are an almost perfect reflection of

The 1940 Pioneer Roadster by Gendron was also referred to as the Skippy Roadster. The neat thing about this model was its opening hood and imitation motor. The cream and red colors really stood out, but it also came in other color combinations. This Gendron model is one of the most sought-after pedal cars today.

Gendron originally manufactured this 1940 Pioneer Skippy Roadster. A cute little car, it came in at least six different color combinations. It also came with either solid or slotted wheels and in the common fire chief version. The deluxe model also came with a windshield and horn. In the late 1940s, Garton came out with a very similar model. This car was not restored to original condition since the rear of the seat has a Garton decal. Also the hood ornament is incorrect. Still, it has a present value of more than $2,000.

the styles, production methods, and even the tone of the auto industry as it evolved throughout the twentieth century. For the early 1940s, pedal cars were doing what they had always done: follow the lead of the real auto makers. By this time, cars had been streamlined, smoothed, and tweaked to the point that they were fantastically reliable, imminently practical, and coming closer to the basics in automotive design that we know today. All this refinement, however, came at the price of some of the grandeur being taken out of the automobile.

Consider that some of the most important technical breakthroughs of the 1940s for the American auto industry were the introduction of the automatic transmission and the refinement of the V-8 engines. While automatic transmissions and smooth V-8s would set the tone for the next three decades in the auto industry, none of these things really grabs the attention, like those massive V-12 and V-16 Goliaths that filled the front fenders of luxury car makers like Cadillac, Lincoln, and Packard.

Automobile styling for the 1940s for the most part, continued to follow the path that had begun the decade before, but the automobile was now a more fluid design than the cars of the 1930s had been. Headlights and

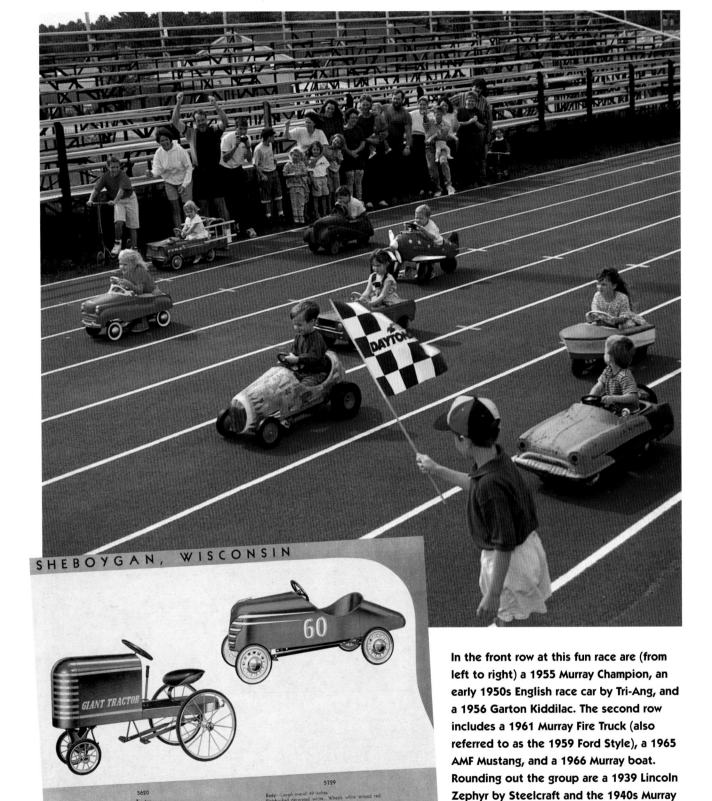

SHEBOYGAN, WISCONSIN

GIANT TRACTOR

60

5620
Tractor
Body—Length overall 43 inches.
Finish—Body red decorated ivory. Seat black. Gear red. Wheels ivory.
Equipment—Adjustable steel spring seat. Towing hitch at rear. Gear shift lever.
Gear—Roller bearing legs and drive shafts at rear.
Wheels—Wire spokes with barrel hub. 8-inch front wheels. 16-inch rear wheels.
Tires—1-inch rubber.
Packing—One in carton.
Weight—49 pounds.

5729
Body—Length overall 49 inches.
Finish—Red decorated white. Wheels white striped red.
Equipment—Radiator ornament.
Gear—Roller bearing drive shafts at rear. Adjustable pedals.
Wheels—9-inch artillery with Hercules bearing of cold rolled steel.
Tires—⅞-inch rubber.
Packing—One in carton.
Weight—34 pounds.
5749
Same as 5729, but equipped with new easy propelling chain type drive.

In the front row at this fun race are (from left to right) a 1955 Murray Champion, an early 1950s English race car by Tri-Ang, and a 1956 Garton Kiddilac. The second row includes a 1961 Murray Fire Truck (also referred to as the 1959 Ford Style), a 1965 AMF Mustang, and a 1966 Murray boat. Rounding out the group are a 1939 Lincoln Zephyr by Steelcraft and the 1940s Murray Pursuit Plane in the third row.

Both this tractor and race car are extremely rare today and will bring top dollar.

It's pedal playtime in this 1940 Pioneer Roadster by Gendron.

taillights were finally incorporated directly into the fenders, doing away with the light as a separate unit. The exaggerated forward-leaning look, accented by the V grille, gave way to a wider, flatter front-end treatment. The use of horizontal radiator trim, started in the late 1930s, only added to the wider appearance of 1940s models. Running boards were shrunk down to the point that they were a mere shadow of their former selves, and in a few years, they were done away with completely.

These new looks for the 1940s meant pedal car producers were going to have to come up with fresh designs if they wanted to

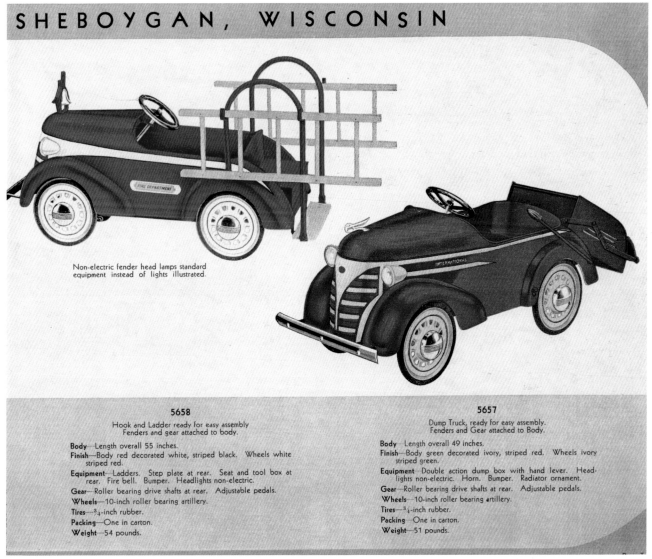

SHEBOYGAN, WISCONSIN

Non-electric fender head lamps standard equipment instead of lights illustrated.

5658
Hook and Ladder ready for easy assembly. Fenders and gear attached to body.

Body—Length overall 55 inches.
Finish—Body red decorated white, striped black. Wheels white striped red.
Equipment—Ladders. Step plate at rear. Seat and tool box at rear. Fire bell. Bumper. Headlights non-electric.
Gear—Roller bearing drive shafts at rear. Adjustable pedals.
Wheels—10-inch roller bearing artillery.
Tires—$\frac{3}{4}$-inch rubber.
Packing—One in carton.
Weight—54 pounds.

5657
Dump Truck, ready for easy assembly. Fenders and Gear attached to Body.

Body—Length overall 49 inches.
Finish—Body green decorated ivory, striped red. Wheels ivory striped green.
Equipment—Double action dump box with hand lever. Headlights non-electric. Horn. Bumper. Radiator ornament.
Gear—Roller bearing drive shafts at rear. Adjustable pedals.
Wheels—10-inch roller bearing artillery.
Tires—$\frac{3}{4}$-inch rubber.
Packing—One in carton.
Weight—51 pounds.

The hook-and-ladder truck and dump truck from the 1940 Garton catalog are variations of the basic 1938 Ford Deluxe.

GARTON TOY COMPANY

5743
Body—Length 48 inches. Rear fenders an integral part of body.
Front fenders welded to body.
Finish—Body maroon decorated ivory. Wheels maroon decorated ivory.
Equipment—Fender head lamps non-electric. Bumper. Buzzer. Luggage compartment. Arm rest. Seat pad.
Gear—Roller bearing drive shafts at rear. Adjustable pedals.
Wheels—9-inch artillery with Hercules bearing of cold rolled steel.
Tires—⅝-inch rubber.
Packing—One in carton.
Weight—48 pounds.

5745
Body—Length 41 inches. Rear fenders an integral part of body.
Front fenders welded to body.
Finish—Body white decorated aluminum, striped red. Windshield, bumper, steering wheel and wheels red.
Equipment—Fender head lamps non-electric. Windshield. Horn. Bumper. Trunk.
Gear—Roller bearing drive shafts at rear. Adjustable pedals.
Wheels—9-inch disc with Hercules bearing of cold rolled steel.
Tires—9-inch puncture proof semi-pneumatic.
Packing—One in carton.
Weight—44 pounds.

The two models shown here from the 1940 Garton catolog are both highly desirable. Either of them would bring $3,000+ on today's market.

keep their offerings looking like the real thing. The Steelcraft line-up for 1940 and 1941 is a good example of the toned-down approach that was beginning to take hold in the pedal car world. The Steelcraft models included Buick, Pontiac, and Chrysler pedal cars, each with a more contemporary horizontal grille, as well as up-to-date trim and headlights. The Buick was finished in red enamel, while the Pontiac was blue; both had white trim. The Chrysler was offered in maroon, blue, or ivory. All these pedal cars had small windshields and rode on solid rubber tires mounted on beaded disc wheels, which were accented with chrome hubcaps. All three were also offered as fire chief's cars, complete with red enamel finish and a fire bell. The Pontiac was produced with an extension on the back that allowed it to be offered in several forms, including a station wagon with metal sides and a tailgate. The wagon was maroon with the extension painted brown. There was also a tow truck offered

This is a 1937 Chrysler Airflow by Steelcraft but it was manufactured in 1941. This body style was made for several years up until the begining of World War II. It is a very distinctive model and is highly desirable—the earlier models are more sought after. In restored condition this 1937 model will bring $3,500 to $4,000+, while a later model will go for $2,500+
Zone Five

with a tow hook mounted in back. It was white with red trim. Finally, there was a red hook and ladder, complete with handrails, ladders, and a bell.

Steelcraft also offered Dodge and Ford pedal cars, but these were somewhat dated when compared to the new body styles of the 1940s. The Dodge was finished in red with white trim, while the Ford was blue with white trim. Both rode on solid rubber tires mounted on artillery wheels, and topped with plated hubcaps. They were also available as fire chief's cars, finished in red, of course. The fire chief versions did away with the windshield and horn but did come equipped with a bell.

The Lincoln Zephyr by Steelcraft was a graceful looking reproduction of its name-sake. With its fine flowing lines, smaller wraparound windshield, and streamlined

lights mounted on top of the front fenders, the Zephyr was available in several versions. There was a base model with solid 10-inch disc wheels. It was offered in maroon enamel with white trim, red enamel with white trim, or brown enamel with orange trim. The next step up, in terms of details and cost, was the Zephyr with two-tone blue enamel finish, red wheels and chrome plating on the windshield frame, steering wheel, front bumper, and headlights. It also featured semipneumatic, puncture-proof whitewalls.

At the top of the heap, in terms of both price and sophistication, was the Zephyr Deluxe. It sported a two-tone black-and-white enamel finish and featured the same chrome trim parts and semipneumatic white walls as the midpriced Zephyr. In addition to its unique two-tone paint scheme of a black body with white hood, the Deluxe offered a

This Pursuit Plane was made between 1941 and 1950 by the Murray Company. A steel cable runs from the drive axle to the propeller shaft, making the propeller revolve as the airplane is in motion. *Zone Five*

"Swiss music box" wind-up radio, as a finishing touch. It was the finest Steelcraft pedal car that money could buy.

Steelcraft also continued to offer its fine Super Charger, which remained unchanged, with its chrome side exhaust, double-leaf bumper, and small raked windshield. The Super Charger Deluxe was finished in black enamel with red trim, accented by a red seat pad. It rode on semipneumatic white walls mounted on red wheels, while the regular Super Charger rode on solid tires mounted on artillery wheels. Both versions had chrome plating on the windshield frame, exhaust pipes, front bumper, and steering wheel. Another of Count de Sakhnoffsky's designs, the Streamliner, was also offered. It featured the smooth, swept-back look, complete with long

Another pedal car illustration in the popular press. This 1944 issue of *The Saturday Evening Post* shows a 1934 Steelcraft on its cover. The A, B, C stickers were for gas rationing during the war years.

lights that stretched down the sides of the hood. The Streamliner was green with a windshield, front bumper, headlights, and artillery wheels finished in ivory.

Another of the Steelcraft offerings of the early 1940s was based on a car that had not been in production as a full-sized automobile for three years. The Chrysler Airflow was finished in maroon with ivory trim and did a fine job of copying the style of the real thing. The Airflow, which was certainly ahead of its time, seemed more in place with the styling of the 1940s than it had when it was introduced by

A Murray Pontiac made between 1941 and 1950. Like the Champion, this model was and still is very popular. This model also came as a tow truck or fire truck. This gold and orange coupe in fairly good original condition today would have a value of around $1,500.

A Pontiac
station wagon
produced by
Murray in the
1940s. *Zone Five*

It's 1947, and little Ron Martin received a brand new red Hamilton Jeep for his birthday. Many other companies had look-a-likes and variations that came as a tow truck, army truck, or fire truck. Some came with a two-position seat to accommodate the child as he or she grew. They also were made with either chain drive or pedal-arm drive, with optional windshield and hood ornament.

Chrysler in 1934. Also included in the Steelcraft line was an Airflow fire truck, complete with ladders, handrails, and a fire bell; and a dump truck with a working dump bed.

The specter of war in Europe came to life in 1939 when Britain and France declared war on Germany, which had stormed into Poland with a vengeance. With the news of war pouring into the country, military toys gained a larger share of the market. Steelcraft's 1940 Army truck and scout plane were a glimpse of what lay ahead in the years to come. The Army truck was built around the Mack fire truck that Steelcraft had offered for several years. In place of the ladders on the fire truck, the military version had a khaki-colored canvas top stretched over removable hoops. It was finished in Hazelwood Brown enamel with orange trim and rode on artillery wheels. The Army scout plane featured the same paint scheme as the Army truck and was detailed with a radial engine, propeller, and wheel guards.

For 1941, Steelcraft's pursuit plane took the military-styled pedal plane in a new, more streamlined and modern direction. The pursuit plane featured a steel body and rode on solid disc wheels. It featured a small windshield, two machine guns, an "aircraft cannon," and a propeller that turned when the plane was pedaled. Two versions of the plane were offered, a U.S. Pursuit Plane, finished in silver with red-and-blue trim, and an Royal Air Force Spitfire, finished in Hazelwood Brown with orange trim.

Gendron offered new, more contemporary versions of its fine Pioneer and Skippy roadsters, with designs based on Fords and Lincolns of the early 1940s. The roadsters featured swept-back fenders, rounded hoods, and streamlined headlights. The finest models had an opening hood that revealed an imitation engine. Some models also had an electric horn, placing them among the few pedal cars equipped with battery-powered accessories during this period. The roadsters were also sold as fire chief's cars, finished in red or white, with lettering and a fire bell.

These fine pedal cars were offered in several colors and trim packages. There were two-tone finishes and aluminum trim parts. The higher-priced offerings had the opening hood and a trim piece on the back to give the appearance of a convertible. All rode on solid rubber tires, some were offered with artillery wheels, and others had solid discs.

Also sold under the roadster name, were the earlier Nash-inspired designs with their forward-leaning V grille, semipneumatic tires, and two-tone finishes. These were big pedal cars that measured 53 inches long and had a shipping weight of 80 pounds. These were also available with electric lights and horns, a rarity for the 1940s.

Gendron also offered a fine fire engine, complete with electric lights, a real rubber hose, and fire bell. There was also a Skippy racer with exposed exhaust running down the side and the popular boat-tail rear-end treatment. It rode on balloon tires

Steelcraft and Murray of Ohio were the same company producing cars under two names. After the war years the name was changed to the Murray Company. This U.S. Pursuit Plane began in 1941 as the Steelcraft Spitfire. It came in hazelwood brown with orange trim and chrome on the propeller, windshield, machine guns, steering wheel, and exhaust. It later was sold in both Air Force and Army models in silver with vermilion and blue trim, and red wheels. The propeller would turn when the plane was pedaled. They were produced from 1941 to 1950.

mounted on ball-bearing disc wheels. There were also several fenderless models available, in a host of body styles, colors, and options.

Garton Manufacturing, which had been producing pedal cars since the early 1900s, had similarly toned-down offerings in its 1940 catalog. Apparently the artwork Garton used was not reflective of the new models being offered for 1940, as the catalog states, "nonelectric fender headlamps standard equipment instead of lights illustrated." Also unusual is the fact that Garton pedal cars, though clearly based on automotive designs of the time, did not identify the cars in its catalog as being styled after a particular auto

manufacturer. Still, the Garton line-up included offerings based on models from Ford, Chevrolet, and other marques.

For 1941, Garton offered several new models, including a roadster, very much like Gendron's 1940 roadster. The Garton roadster was available in two versions. The base model was finished in blue enamel with red fenders and trim. The bumpers and hubcaps were chrome plated. The more upscale roadster featured the opening hood with mock engine and padded armrests. It was finished in maroon enamel with ivory trim.

Garton also offered a pair of station wagons: a base model without fenders or a front

A 1948 Pontiac wrecker by Murray. It has a neat airplane hood ornament and distinctive grille. Many other models were based on this car. *Zone Five*

This special D-4 Cat Bulldozer was made as a promotion for the Caterpillar Tractor Co. Today's value is $2,500+.

bumper finished in tan and trimmed in maroon, and a Mercury model with front and rear fenders and a plated front bumper. It was finished in maroon with ivory trim. Both station wagons had wooden sides and a wood step at the rear. They rode on artillery wheels with solid rubber tires.

Garton's military-inspired pedal cars included the U.S. Army Medical Corps Ambulance, which featured a canvas cover over the rear of the truck. It was finished in khaki with white-and-black trim. It had front and rear fenders and rode on solid rubber tires mounted on artillery wheels. The U.S. Army Tank Division Scout Car was another version, well

equipped with a turret-mounted machine gun that shot "harmless sparks," and an antitank gun on the rear. Other guns were painted on the side of the turret. The Scout Car was finished in khaki with white-and-black trim and rode on artillery wheels. There was also a Garton dive bomber pedal plane.

On December 7, 1941, life in the United States changed for everyone. The Japanese bombed the naval base at Pearl Harbor, Hawaii, and America was plunged into World War II against the Axis powers. America's commitment to the war effort was total, and manufacturing companies of all kinds put aside their regular business and began

The Murray U.S.
Pursuit Plane.

Ed Pert of
Penobscot,
Maine, was four
years old seen
here driving his
1948 Pontiac
station wagon by
Murray. The color
was maroon with
white trim.

producing war goods. Pedal car makers were soon turning out all types of wheeled goods, including hospital gurneys and wheel chairs, as well as stamped metal goods like rifle magazines. Production of pedal cars (and most other toys) ceased from 1942 until after World War II came to a close in August 1945.

Among the companies that retooled for World War II, American National would not go back to producing pedal cars when peace returned. American National had already undergone a major reorganization in 1939, an attempt to stem rising losses in the children's toy business. After the war, the company continued to produce medical devices like gurneys and wheelchairs. American National and its sister companies, Gendron and Toledo, were through with the pedal car business for good. From the turn of the century, the companies that made up American National had produced some the of finest pedal cars ever offered. Now those names, like Skippy, Blue Streak, and Pioneer, would be part of the toy world's past.

While American National was leaving the pedal car business, at least one new company was ready to join the ranks of miniature auto manufacturers. BMC, short for Binghamton Manufacturing Company, was based in Binghamton, New York. While trying to diversify its manufacturing efforts, BMC added pedal cars to its production line in the late 1940s.

In the years immediately following the war, auto makers simply spruced up their prewar offerings and turned them loose on a public eager to buy any new car that found its way into a showroom. Auto manufacturers didn't bother to create new cars. Why should they, when they were selling every car they could produce? Also, there were government price controls in effect that limited the amount of money auto makers could charge the car-starved public for their wares. Staying with the old tried-and-true styles certainly made sense to GM, Ford, and Chrysler.

But while the nation's biggest auto makers may have been satisfied churning out as many cars as they could after the war, there were other auto makers who were still trying to compete with the giants. Among them was Studebaker, which was looking for any advantage it could get over its formidable competition. As the nation got back to the business of

Another superb advertisement. The pedal car is a 1936 Ford by Steelcraft.

making and buying cars, Studebaker found an advantage in its relatively small size. It was far easier for a company as small as Studebaker to offer an entirely new model. So, in 1947, Studebaker proudly released the Champion. The company touted its all-new design with the slogan "the first by far with a postwar car," which was not only catchy, but true. In a few years, Murray Ohio would put the Champion name on one of its new pedal cars.

The new Studebaker, and other new offerings from independent auto makers that would soon follow it, were more smooth and rounded than previous designs. Fenders, which had gone from a separate design element to the pontoon look of the late 1930s, were now even less obtrusive than they had been. In the case of the Studebaker, the sides of the body were somewhat swollen in appearance. Slab-sided, though an unflattering

"Congratulations on your new home." The Buick Woodie wagon is by the Tri-Ang Co. from England and the 1935 Pontiac Skippy is from the Gendron Co. of Ohio. The happy children are Courtney Wright, Eric Folmer, and Travis Poulin.

term, is one of the ways these new postwar designs have been described. The Studebaker also offered a unique wraparound rear window, which was quite popular with several designers, in the front and the rear for many years to come.

Model year 1949 was a watershed for American automotive manufacturers, as Chevrolet, Ford, and Chrysler all finally found the time to offer completely new automobiles for the first time since 1941. The heavy, slab-sided look was everywhere. The extruding fender was in full retreat. Cars such as the Chevrolets and Chryslers still had a hint of fender bulging out at the rear of the

car, but that would disappear shortly. Headlights now rested on the front of the car at the top of the fender line. Chrome started to make a big, big comeback. Many finer grille and trim pieces were replaced by large, heavy chrome trim parts.

For 1949, it was also time to offer new pedal car designs. Every auto maker had restyled, so if the pedal car makers wanted to keep their models looking current, they had to follow suit. The trend toward simplifying designs also continued. Fewer pedal cars offered the detailing and accessories that were seen in the years before the war. The public had waited a long time for the chance to buy

The Comet by Murray of Ohio was produced in 1949 and 1950. This car was sometimes referred to as a Mercury. Its rich maroon finish with silver trim and bright red wheels had the eye appeal to attract every youngster. It also came in standard, deluxe, and a fire chief model. It had the same body style used for the Murray's Torpedo model.

new toys of any kind, so sophistication was not as important as it had once been. The faster pedal cars could be made, the faster they could be sold to people who had waited for years for things to get back to normal. Fewer body styles were offered, fewer options were offered, and at the time very few people seemed to mind.

Murray, which had produced Steelcraft pedal cars for many years, was set with a great line-up for 1949. From now on, the pedal car line would be known as Murray, with the Steelcraft name retired. Murray's Torpedo, which took its name and "porthole" trim at the top of the fenders from the Buick Roadmaster, was ready to wow kids and parents who had seen the new Buick. The Murray Comet was a fine-looking postwar car that shared a name with Mercury. The Comet's thicker, heavier look, with flatter, or slab sides and a smaller grille opening was right with the times. The Comet was also offered as the ever-popular fire chief's car, complete with a fire bell. Murray also brought back its 1941 Pontiac models, as a car, station wagon, and fire truck.

The 1949 Garton models weren't quite up to speed with the new looks just yet. Garton also continued to produce catalogs that didn't name its pedal cars after the real cars that had inspired them. There was a pedal car with Nash-inspired, forward V nose lacked fenders. This simple pedal car was offered as both a passenger car and a fire chief's car complete with fire bell. Its appearance was rather dated, in light of the new wider, lower offerings that were now the standard of automotive design. There was also a pedal car based on Ford, as well as a Woody station wagon.

For all their success at capturing the contemporary look of late 1940s, these pedal cars were seriously lacking detail compared to previous efforts. The accessories, the interior detail, the opening hoods or trunks were all gone. Battery-powered lights or horns, which had mostly fallen out of favor before the war, also did not return. Two-tone paint schemes had gone out of vogue with most auto manufacturers, but could be seen on pedal cars for the time being. Trim parts, once plated in nickel and later chrome, were now more likely to be painted white or silver. Wheels, which earlier had been wire spokes, or the artillery type, would go back to being solid discs, often with no hubcap to dress them up. Still, pedal cars had returned, and the public accepted them without any complaints.

"Hitch your sales to a star"

AMILTON'S ORIGINAL

ODEL NO. 800* MODEL NO. 800CD

AIR FORCE JEEP
and Army Jeep

Now better than ever before.

✪ New low price.

✪ New luxury wheels with semi-pneumatic tire

✪ New shorter turning radius.

✪ New pre-assembled chassis.

✪ These Jeeps bear authentic Air
markings in red, white, and blue.
are timely, realistic toys loaded
play value. The Hamilton Air
Jeep is a proven business buile

Still the

best seller .

SPECIFICATIONS
Easy assembly
Sturdy, welded steel construction
Ball bearing rear axle, push rods and wheels
Baked enamel, Official Air Force Blue
Realistic markings
Two seat levels, three pedal adjustments
Front and rear bumpers
Large 8" wheels, semi-pneumatic 1¼" tires
Press-on permanent locking hub caps
Model 803: Same car with Army markings

SHIPPING INFORMATION
Packed one to a carton 16⅛" x 20⅛"
Running gear pre-assembled
Shipping weight: 36 lbs.

Equipped with Steel Linked Chain D

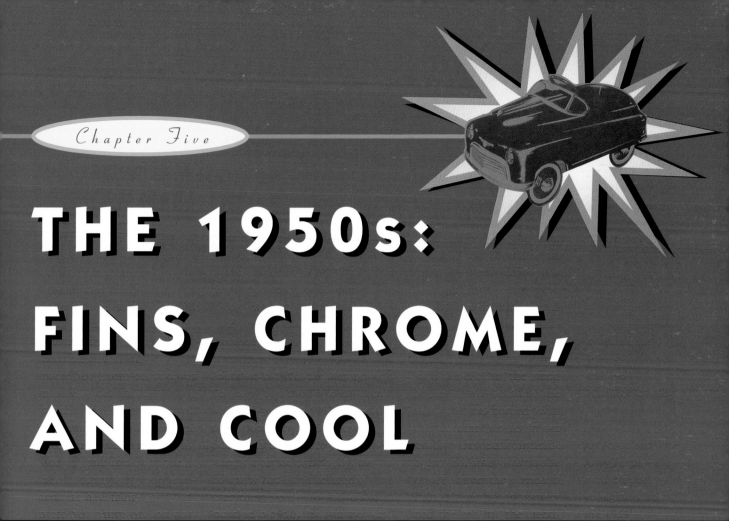

Chapter Five

THE 1950s: FINS, CHROME, AND COOL

With auto makers finally offering the public new models for the first time in nearly a decade, pedal car manufacturers had their work cut out for them in 1950. Automotive design, which for the years immediately following World War II had consisted mainly of creating new trim parts to hang on prewar models, was in full swing again. Pedal car makers, still committed to following the latest automotive designs, had to get busy. That meant new tooling was being readied, new catalogs and ads were being printed, and new

MURRAY O. CLEVE. O.

Founded in 1910, the Murray Company branched into children's wheeled-goods in 1923. It was the parent company of Steelcraft pedal cars until 1973. Called Murray International today, the company has manufactured everything from automotive sheet metal to bicycles to lawn mowers.

life had been pumped into the pedal car business. Along with this growth, a new manufacturing giant took its place among the pedal car makers of the 1950s.

In the next two decades, the steel-bodied pedal car would make its last stand. Plastic was on the horizon, and it would ultimately spell the end for the metal-bodied pedal car. Besides that, the fascination with the automobile itself was simply not what it once had been. For the ultimate in travel adventure, people turned their heads skyward and looked to the moon

Air Force and Army Jeeps were available for youngsters from the 1959 Hamilton catalog.

81

A 1950 Murray Comet and a 1950 Murray Champion. *Zone Five*

For the early 1950s, cars were lower, straighter, and wider. While the slab-sided look had taken hold quickly, designers began tinkering with it almost immediately. When they did, their attention turned to chrome. Maybe it was the postwar years, when new trim pieces were hung on existing designs, or maybe it was the fact that the bigger, flatter bodies proved to be the perfect canvas to display all kinds of ornamental pieces. Whatever the reason, the trim parts were shiny and big, and they kept getting bigger. Ford's all-new postwar models had a large, round chrome "pie pan" or "nose cone," depending on your imagination and taste, right in the middle of the grille.

Pedal car makers tried to stay right on the heels of the late 1940s redesigns, which replaced earlier models that began life before World War II started. The timing was perfect. The war years were finally put to rest, the new cars created a new sense of excitement in the automotive world, and the new pedal cars were in the right place at the right time to take full advantage.

and the stars beyond. Before they faded away, however, the pedal car makers did stage a bit of a comeback. Though they were nowhere near as detailed as the fine pedal cars of the glory years of the 1920s and 1930s, the 1950s would see a bit of a revival in features like battery-powered lights and horns, interiors with more detail, and even two-tone paint jobs.

Havin' Fun THE **REAL** ROY ROGERS WAY!

HI, KIDS! ALL THE COWPOKES IN THIS PICTURE WITH ME ARE WEARING MY DOUBLE R BAR CLOTHES. THEIR GUNS AND HOLSTERS ARE REAL ROY ROGERS, TOO! IF YOU'D LIKE TO OWN ANYTHING YOU SEE HERE, TELL MOM THAT EVERYTHING IS SOLD AT ALL GOOD DEPARTMENT STORES.

Roy Rogers

LOOK FOR MY DOUBLE R BRAND

on archery sets • action toys • banks • bed spreads • billfolds • belts • books • boots • chap-vest sets • chuckwagons • gloves • guns • guitars • hats • holsters • horseshoe sets • jackets • jigsaw puzzles • jeans • lanterns • lunch kits • jewelry • pajamas • paint and crayon coloring sets • pencil tablets • records • robes • raincoats • ranch models • Roy and Trigger models • shirts • school bags • saddle seats • slipper sox • slacks • stuffed toys • suits • sweaters • tents • toy stagecoaches • ties • watches.

While the new models helped pump life back into the pedal car business, pedal car manufacturers had slimmed down their offerings. New body styles were created that replaced the prewar offerings, but the selection of pedal cars was nowhere near the level it had been before the war. In addition, the names of the cars started to be centered on specific models and not the manufacturers themselves. As the decade continued, the emphasis on keeping up with current automotive designs would start to fade, and pedal car manufacturers would even find inspiration for new designs from sources other than the auto makers.

Murray wasted no time in jumping on the big, rounded band wagon with several new offerings. The Champion, named after the Studebaker of 1947, was a simple, unadorned little pedal car that was finished in light blue and rode on solid disc, ball bearing wheels, and featured a minimum of detail

and trim parts. While the Studebaker design of the same name didn't last, the Champion certainly did. It was a low-priced pedal car that proved to be enormously popular with the buying public. It also was put into service, with an extension on the back, as a fire truck. Finished in red, the fire truck had a hinged rear gate, fire bell, and a pair of ladders. It was also offered as a station wagon, with a green body and white trim.

Another new series of Murray pedal trucks, with their large, silver-painted front bumper and grille trim captured the look of the heavy trim parts that 1950s automotive designers were producing. Because of the down-turned look of the grille, these pedal trucks are now commonly referred to as the "Sad Face" design. There was a dump truck, with working dump bed and a bulb horn, finished in red enamel. The station wagon featured a steel extension with working tailgate

The Nellybelle Jeep by Hamilton Co. was introduced in the early 1950s. Because of its association with Roy Rogers, it is even more collectable today. An excellent original or correctly restored Nellybelle Jeep would sell today for around $1,500.

and handrails finished in maroon enamel. The fire truck came ready for action with fire bell and ladders, and it was finished in red. All these vehicles were powered by pedal drive and rode on solid disc wheels.

The prewar Pontiac design was still being offered as a car, station wagon, and fire truck. All three featured small windshields, pedal drive, and beaded solid disc wheels. The car and station wagon were blue with white trim, while the fire engine was, of course, red with white trim and came with the ever-popular fire bell and ladders. The Comet, which also featured the new lower rounded look, complete with slab sides was a hit. The Torpedo took its primary styling mark from the "porthole" trim on the fenders of the Buick Roadmaster, which gave pedal car buyers a chance to own the junior version of a car that was well received for its styling.

For Garton Manufacturing, 1950 was the year the company rolled out a pedal car that captured the most famous styling element of the 1950s. The tailfin was on its way

to becoming an American automotive icon, and the Garton Kidillac proudly sported a pair of fins, just like its namesake. When the Cadillac received its postwar redesign in 1948, a year ahead of most GM cars, it featured a pair of fins at the end of the rear fenders, said to be inspired by the P-38 fighter plane of World War II. This was a totally new look, and it proved to be prophetic. As the jet and rocket captured the imagination of the public, the fin was in, and Cadillac had the biggest fins of all, growing to amazing heights on the 1959 Eldorado.

The Garton Kidillac featured the first generation of tailfin, a mere suggestion of the fins that would follow. The Kidillac was available in three versions. There was a base model, finished in maroon with white trim, and the fire chief's car, complete with decals and a fire bell and finished in an appropriate shade of red. Both these cars featured standard pedal drive and rode on solid rubber tires mounted on disc wheels. The third Kidillac

Race cars are highly desirable collectibles today. This No. 5 from the Italian company Giordani is no exception. Today's market could bring $2,500+.

was most notable for its use of chain drive. According to Ed Weirick, chain drive was added to make the cars easier to pedal. The chain drive Kidillac was blue with white trim and rode on the same tires and wheels as the other two models.

Garton also produced a flat-faced model that lacked fenders. This simple pedal car was powered by pedal drive and rode on the same tires and wheels as the Kidillac. It was available as a car finished in green and trimmed in white. With its battery-powered spotlight and siren, the police car version offered a little more detailing and excitement. The police car, finished in white with black-and-red trim, also sported an adjustable radio antenna. Finally, there was a fire truck finished in red with white trim. It included a fire bell and a pair of ladders.

Garton also continued to offer the woody station wagon and fire truck based on their earlier designs with styling elements

The IH-Farmall midsize tractor was produced in the 1950s by Eska, which is now owned by Ertl Co. in Dyersville, Iowa. Pedal tractors are in demand today more than ever and many of the aluminum open-motor styles will bring top dollar. Note the high steering and closed grill. *Zone Five*

SNOW PLOW

Metal Blade and holding bar with metal extension arm for affixing to front of tractor. An extra sand mover in summer, snow plow in winter. Wt. 4 lbs.

B-865

FIRE FIGHTER

Contains two wooden ladders plus a platform and hoop handles that enable a child to ride standing up. Has a bright nickel plated bell—looks like a real hook and ladder. Wt. 14 lbs.

B-400

from Ford. Both of these pedal cars had front and rear fenders and featured the older look of the prewar designs. The headlights were mounted on the front fenders, and the grille was the popular V shape. Both had chromed front bumpers and were powered by pedal drive. The station wagon was maroon with white trim and featured a real wooden extension and front and rear seats. The fire engine was decked out in red, complete with a pair of ladders, chrome handrails, and fire bell.

BMC, which began pedal car production after the war, was also producing pedal cars that captured the slab-sided look of the cars of the day. The BMC line-up included pedal cars, tractors, bicycles, and tricycles. The BMC racer series was one of the few pedal cars of the period that found

BMC (Binghamton Manufacturing Corporation) only lasted from 1944 until 1954, but it made some great attachments and accessories.

A 1953 Murray dump truck—also referred to as the Sad Face. Besides the well-known yellow model, another popular color was two-tone highway orange with black trim. Some of the models had a gear shift with a realistic motor tone.

There's Nellybelle again. The popular Jeep is both a hot Roy Rogers collectible as well as a pedal car collectible.

its inspiration in race car designs.

In a few years, it was time for another set of redesigns in the automotive world. The initial postwar redesigns from the late 1940s were gone rather quickly. In their place were cars that were a bit shorter, more squared off, and lower. The wraparound windshield and rear window found more acceptance, and chrome trim parts continued to grow in size and weight. Ford redesigned first, in 1952, followed by Chevrolet, Chrysler, Cadillac, and others in 1953. Cadillac's biggest news was the Eldorado convertible, a car that would help lay the groundwork for the excess that would soon follow. The Eldorado featured a wraparound windshield, more defined tailfins, and large chrome "bullets" on the front and rear bumpers.

Not to be outdone, at least in the outrageous styling department, Studebaker, which helped introduce the new postwar look with its Champion in 1947, went one better and

SALES STIMULATOR

The "Taxi" hood ornament and meter box will delight the young cab driver.

TAXI

Pedal Drive Model 704

DIMENSIONS: Length 35", width 18".

FEATURES: Spare wheel and tire on rear. "Taxi" hood ornament. Simulated meter box and flag.

DRIVE: Pedal drive with ball bearings in pull straps.

PEDALS: Can be adjusted to three positions.

TIRES: 7½" x ⅝" solid rubber.

SEAT PAD: Tough fiber.

FINISH: Yellow with black trim. Yellow wheels. Black steering wheel and seat pad. Bumpers, headlamps and hub caps are painted silver.

PACKING: One per carton.

SHIPPING WEIGHT: Approximately 29 lbs.

F.O.B. BINGHAMTON, N. Y.

An all-original or correctly restored mid-1950s BMC taxi would sell today for $1,000+.

pedal car makers turned out their versions of the slab-sided postwar designs, and came up with new offerings that found their inspiration in places other than the auto makers. On the whole, details and frills were starting to return to some pedal cars. Battery-powered lights and horns made a come back on the more elaborate models. Chain drive became more common after pedal drive had been the most popular means of power for many years. Plastic, too, started to show up on some pedal car trim parts. Nylon inserts in wheels were touted for the smoothness and durability they provided.

BMC offered several different lines of pedal cars, including the Blue Streak series, the Challenger series, Thunderbolt series, Jet Liner series, and a line of pedal tractors, simply called the Tractor series. The pedal cars were built on three body styles that were all postwar slab-sided models. The Challenger series included a station wagon, a dump truck, and a hook and ladder that featured an extension on the rear of the car to make it into a truck.

The Jet Liner series also offered a standard convertible, along with the station wagon, dump truck, and hook and ladder truck that were created by adding a steel extension onto the back of the basic car design. The tractor series featured at least two designs offered in different variations, and they all rode on solid rubber tires and were powered by pedal drive. There were also several implements available for the tractors, including a front end scoop, a cart, and a plow.

BMC offered its Racer series, based on the open-wheel race cars of the day. The Racers had the long-nose, short-tail look of cars

unleashed its wild bullet nose on the world in 1950 and 1951. Chrome took center stage, quite literally, with introduction of the bullet-nose Studebakers, which featured a large chrome medallion in the middle of the grille that dominated the front end of the car.

This design pushed the limits and sensibilities of the buying public, but Studebaker, in a desperate fight for survival, seemed to be willing to roll the dice. Giordani of Italy, which had resumed pedal car production following World War II, produced a pedal car version of this famous, or infamous, design. Studebaker stuck with the bullet look for only a couple of years, going on to other designs, ranging from flashy to drab, before calling it quits in 1966.

In a few years after the start of the 1950s,

ACCESSORIES

BELLS

Streamlined Nickel Plated Bell and Bracket Assembly. This Bell is standard equipment on all BMC Fire Chiefs, Hook and Ladders, and Fire Fighter.

C-200-46

SIREN

Polished finish. Pump type, operated by hand. This will make the Fire Fighter even more thrilling to the youngsters, and will afford greater play value. Easily attached.

B-412

Just a few of the pedal car accessories that are so sought after today. Many nice reproductions are being made, but the real original items make today's restorations extra special.

FOR THUNDERBOLT AUTO ONLY. A real trailer hitch, to which attachments may be hooked. Two pierced holes at back of auto for securing the hitch. Multiplies play value, as youngster can use any of the pull attachments illustrated, including the Trailer, Fire Fighter, Wrecker, Sulky, Grader or Dump Cart.

C-262

For front of tractor. Uses Standard Flashlight batteries (not furnished). Metal case. Brackets and bolts for attaching. Plastic lens.

B-860

Available for BMC Autos. Brightly colored in yellow and black. Is only available reading U. S. A. 78762.

C-265

In 1955 these Murray tractors sold for $10 to $12 each.

that competed in open-wheel competitions on dirt tracks and famous venues like the Indianapolis Motor Speedway. The Racers featured a long, straight exhaust pipe that ran down the side of the car, a hand brake (non-working), and were numbered for further authenticity. They rode on semipneumatic tires mounted on disc wheels and were powered by pedal drive.

Garton Manufacturing continued to offer their Kidillac in several versions. There was a Police Chief finished in black, with a battery-powered spotlight, bulb horn, and an aerial. The Fire Chief was white with red trim and had a fire bell and the same battery-powered spotlight as the police model. The standard Kidillac was dressed up with a rearview mirror and continental-style spare tire mounted on the rear bumper.

Taking pedal cars into the space race was Garton's Space Cruiser, a three-wheeled design, with one front and two rear wheels. The Space Cruiser had the bullet nose of a rocket, with an adjustable saddle seat and pod-like fenders that covered the rear wheels. It was powered by chain drive and rode on solid rubber tires. The Space Cruiser came complete with a toy space gun that

L-301

Specifications same as L-302 except: Pedal drive, color red, weight 31 lbs. Has gear shift lever.

L-302

CHAIN DRIVE MURRAY TRAC WITH MOTOR-TONE SHIFT

S P E C I F I C A T I O N S	
C O N S T R U C T I O N	
DIMENSIONS: Length 38½", width 20½", height 27½"	**CHAIN GUARD:** Steel, attractively designed, chain enclosed
FRAME: 1¼" tubular, heavy gauge steel, hydrogen brazed	**CHAIN:** Standard bicycle roller type
HOOD: Heavy gauge steel, tractor type, with gear shift lever	**TIRES:** 1¼" semi-pneumatic front and rear. Rear tires have tractor tread
SEAT: All steel, adjustable	
WHEELS: 8" ball bearing front, 10" rear	**F I N I S H**
DRIVING MECHANISM: Ball bearing chain drive mechanism. Pedal crank rotates in a ball bearing hanger	Body in Highway Orange with Black trim. Seat and steering wheel Black. Wheels, Highway Orange
STEERING MECHANISM: Universal joint allowing 360° turning	**P A C K I N G**
GEAR SHIFT: Plastic, realistic motor-tone	One per carton. Shipping weight 34 lbs.

Pure elegance is the only way to describe this car, which originally was built as a 1955 Lancer by Murray. This car was restored and customized (as a 1955 Belair) with nearly 300 hours of labor and research. Some of the features are: stainless steel moldings, a recessed steering wheel and horn ring, a handmade dash, direction and gear shift levers, dual exhaust, a continental kit, hood ornament, fuzzy dice, working miniature tools in the trunk, a full interior, radio antenna, and factory colors.

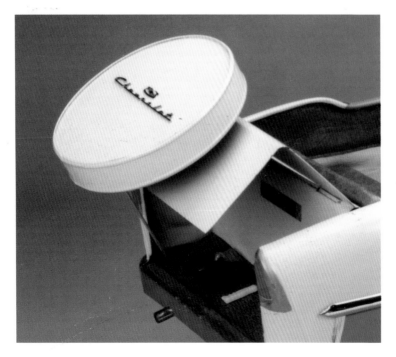

fired plastic projectiles.

Murray's answer to the space race was the Super Sonic Jet and the Sky Rocket. Both had three-wheel designs that seem to be derived from pedal tractor layouts. The Super Sonic Jet was powered by chain drive and finished in Stratosphere Blue with Rocket Red trim. It had a detailed instrument panel, dual stick controls mounted in the cockpit, and a motor tone shift mounted on the fuselage on the driver's side. The Sky Rocket was similar, with the same body, finished in Rocket Red with Stratosphere Blue trim.

Murray found more inspiration away from automotive design with its three-wheeled motorcycles. The Murray Good Humor Truck and Police Cycle were introduced in 1955. They were powered by chain drive, and featured a motorcycle-inspired front end,

These models by Murray are some of the most popular from the 1950s.

Model L-612 — Royal De Luxe
Dyna Chain Drive with Motor Tone Shift
Full Ball Bearing

DIMENSIONS: Length 36", width 17"
WHEELS: 8", double disc
DRIVING MECHANISM: Ball bearing chain drive mechanism
GEAR SHIFT: Plastic, Realistic Motor-Tone
CONTINENTAL SPARE WHEEL: ⅝" solid rubber 8" double disc
RADIATOR ORNAMENT: Bright plated
WINDSHIELD: Aluminum
TIRES: ⅝" solid rubber
FINISH: Body two-tone Bittersweet and Castle Tan. Wheels in Castle Tan with Black stripe
PACKING: One per carton. Shipping wt. 32 lbs.

Model L-621 — Fire Truck
Full Ball Bearing

DIMENSIONS: Length 43", width 17"
WHEELS: Ball bearing, 8" double disc
DRIVING MECHANISM: Ball bearing pull straps, ball bearing rear axle hangers
FIRE CHIEF BELL: Bright plated
HAND RAILS: Steel
LADDERS: Wooden
TIRES: ⅝" solid rubber
FINISH: Body in two-tone vermilion and white baked enamel, side panels vermilion, yellow trim, Silver enameled grille.
PACKING: One per carton. Shipping wt. 34 lbs.

Model L-611 — Fire Chief
Ball Bearing Construction

DIMENSIONS: Length 36", width 17"
WHEELS: 8", double disc
DRIVING MECHANISM: Ball bearing pull straps, ball bearing rear axle hangers
BELL: Bright plated
TIRES: ⅝" solid rubber
FINISH: Body in vermilion baked enamel with white trim, Silver enameled grille
PACKING: One per carton. Shipping wt. 28 lbs.

A 1955 Murray dump truck in yellow with black trim. Smiling in the driver seat is Ellen Casion from Marieha, South Carolina. Forty years later Ellen sent co-author Ed Weirick the same dump truck to be restored. This body style is also referred to as the Sad Face because of the way the grille is shaped.

Model L-610 — Champion
Ball Bearing Construction

DIMENSIONS: Length 36", width 17"
WHEELS: 8", double disc
DRIVING MECHANIISM: Ball bearing pull straps, ball bearing rear axle hangers
RADIATOR ORNAMENT: Bright plated
TIRES: ⅝" solid rubber
FINISH: Body in Acacia Blue baked enamel with dark blue trim and silver enameled grille
PACKING: One per carton. Shipping wt. 28 lbs.

complete with gas tank and a bench seat that included an enclosed storage compartment. The Good Humor Truck was finished in white, with bright blue trim on the gas tank and wheels. It was finished with a silver grille and exhaust pipe, "Good Humor" and "Ice Cream" decals, and a plated bell. The Police Radar Patrol cycle was finished in blue with white trim and came with a working mechanical siren and an antenna.

Murray's Sad Face series of trucks were available in several variations. The dump

Ed Weirick's Maine antique shop is home to many different pedal cars. This 1955 Murray fire chief car was restored by Ed. Its value today is more than $1,500.

A Murray 1955 tractor and dump trailer. Tractors are becoming more and more sought after by collectors, and this model is no exception. It had features such as an adjustable gear shift and a dumping mechanism for the trailer. Value in restored condition would be $700 for the tractor and $150 for the trailer.

truck featured a chain drive, two-tone orange-and-black finish, and a noise-making shifter. The dump bed could be operated by a lever while the driver was still seated. The Ranch Wagon was a two-toned station wagon finished in two shades of green that were clearly inspired by the automotive colors of the day. The fire truck was two-tone red and white, with a pair of ladders, handrails, and a fire bell. Both the dump truck and ranch wagon were powered by pedal drive.

Murray's popular Champion was offered in several variations, the nicest of which was the Royal Deluxe. Powered by chain drive, and sporting a two-tone brown-and-tan finish, the Royal Deluxe had a continental-styled spare tire mounted to the rear of the body. The grille trim was plated and the windshield was made of aluminum. The Fire Chief Champion sported a red finish, fire bell, and the appropriate decals. The Fire Truck had a metal extension added to the back of the Champion body. It was white with red-and-yellow trim and had a pair of ladders and a fire bell. The standard Champion was blue with dark blue trim and a silver

enamel grille. All the pedal cars based on the Champion design except for the Royal Deluxe were powered by pedal drive.

The automotive designers, apparently still restless after the lull in design work during World War II, offered new designs again in 1955. This time around, the auto designers hit their mark in ways that few others in their profession have. The cars they created during the mid-1950s have become icons of American automotive design. Tailfins were everywhere, as was wraparound glass. Chrome was still growing in size, and new mechanical improvements in engine and sus-

A 1956 Garton Fire Dept. Ladder Truck. This model also came as the Fire Chief, Mark V, Dragnet, etc., and in a variation of colors and graphics. Production ran into the early 1960s. Restored value today is $700.+

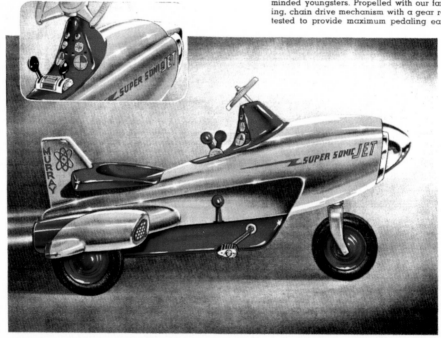

SUPER SONIC JET DYNA-CHAIN DRIVE
FULL BALL BEARING

NEW! MOTOR-TONE SHIFT LEVER AND REALISTIC DUAL JET CONTROLS

THE SUPER SONIC JET. A design of tomorrow for space minded youngsters. Propelled with our famous ball bearing, chain drive mechanism with a gear ratio thoroughly tested to provide maximum pedaling ease.

L-900

One look says it all: 1950s. The original price for this jet in the 1955 Murray catalog was $15.82. Today it would fetch $1,200+.

S P E C I F I C A T I O N S	
C O N S T R U C T I O N	**CHAIN GUARD:** Encloses chain for safety
DIMENSION: Length 45", wing spread 25"	**CONTROLS:** Realistic Dual Jet Controls—Simulated gauges and instruments
MATERIAL: Heavy gauge steel body and undergear	**GEAR SHIFT:** Plastic, realistic motor-tone **REFLECTOR:** Jeweled
WHEELS: 8" double disc, ball bearing	**SPINNER AND JET INTAKE NOSE:** Chrome plated
TIRES: 1¾" semi-pneumatic	**F I N I S H**
DRIVING MECHANISM: Chain drive, ball bearing crank hanger and rear axle mountings. Drive ratio affords maximum pedaling ease.	Fuselage and delta wing Stratosphere Blue. Rudders, wheels, chain guard, and other trim in Rocket Red.
CHAIN: Standard bicycle roller type	**P A C K I N G**
STEERING MECHANISM: Universal joint 360° turn. Full sleeve head bearing	One per carton — Weight 42 lbs.

JUVENILE WHEEL GOODS

BMC MANUFACTURING CORP., BINGHAMTON, NEW YORK • Subsidiary of American Machine & Foundry Company, New York

MODEL A-622
SUPER JET CONVERTIBLE
Two Speed Speed-O-Matic Chain Drive

Dimensions—Length 37", width 19". **Styling**—New sports car grille, louvered hood. Deluxe rear end. **Drive**—Two speed. Shifts from low ratio (1 to 1) to high (2 to 1). Impossible to strip gears. Speed-O-Matic drive combines reciprocal action of pedal drive and geared ratio of chain drive. **Tires**—8" x ⅝" solid rubber. **Bearings**—Ball bearing construction. **Seat Pad**—Tough fiber. White. **Finish**—Metallic wine red body. White wheels, steering wheel, windshield and lettering. Silver painted grille and tail lights. Plated headlamps. **Packing**—One per carton. **Shipping Weight**—Approximately 36 lbs.

MODEL A-631
SUPER SPORT CONVERTIBLE
Speed-O-Matic Chain Drive

Dimensions—Length 37", width 19". **Styling**—New sports car grille, louvered hood. Deluxe rear end. **Speed-O-Matic Drive**—Combination of pedal and chain type drive combines reciprocal motion of pedal drive and geared ratio of chain drive. **Bearings**—Ball bearing construction. **Wheels**—Simulated wire wheels with 7½" x 1¼" semi-pneumatic tires. **Trim**—Plated hub caps and headlamps. **Finish**—Metallic blue body. Red seat pad. White steering wheel, lettering, wheels and windshield. Silver painted grille. **Tail Lights**—Bright red plastic, simulated. **Exhausts**—Black rubber, simulated. **Packing**—One per carton. **Shipping Weight**—Approximately 34 lbs.

MODEL A-634
SPORTLINER STATION WAGON
Speed-O-Matic Chain Drive

Dimensions—Length 42½", width 19". **Styling**—New sports car grille, louvered hood. **Speed-O-Matic Drive**—Combination of pedal and chain type drive combines reciprocal motion of pedal drive and geared ratio of chain drive. **Bearings**—Ball bearing construction. **Wheels**—Simulated wire wheels with 7½" x 1¼" semi-pneumatic tires. **Rear Box**—Large capacity, for carrying toys, etc. Heavy gauge steel hand rails. **Trim**—Plated hub caps and headlamps. **Finish**—Hawaiian bronze body. Ivory steering wheel, windshield, hand rails, wheels and trim on sides and seat. Silver painted grille. **Packing**—One per carton. **Shipping Weight**—Approximately 35 lbs.

AMF took over BMC in 1954 and used the same body for a few years. This is the only model known with a louvered hood.

pension design provided more power and a smoother ride. Chevrolet sales sky rocketed with its 1955 designs and new V-8 engines. Ford and Chrysler didn't fair too poorly either, as auto manufacturers created cars that were well received by the public.

While no pedal car maker actually produced a 1955–1957 Chevrolet for the public, a 1955 model was produced for promotional purposes for Chevrolet. Ed Weirick, taking matters into his own hands, customized a Murray Lancer to create a 1955 Chevrolet in turquoise and cream. Ed was one of the first pedal car fans to create a pedal car version of the classic Chevys from the mid-1950s, and the idea has proved quite popular with pedal car lovers since that time.

In the pedal car world, there was big news as well. BMC seemed to be doing quite well in children's wheel goods. Though relatively new, having introduced their offerings after World War II, BMC had a healthy line-up of bicycles, tricycles, and pedal cars. Everything was going well. So well, in fact, that BMC sold its children's wheeled goods business to manufacturing giant AMF. Best known for its Bowling equipment, AMF, which stood for American Machine & Foundry, was a huge manufacturing company whose product lines were so diverse, they seemed to have little in common, save for the fact that they were owned by AMF and they turned a profit. As a big company, AMF did things in a big way. So, when it wanted to get in to the pedal car business, the company simply bought one of the country's largest producers of pedal cars.

Now that the field was set with Murray, Garton, AMF, and a few smaller manufacturers, the pedal car business heated up again.

A 1956 Murray Dip Side fire chief car. One can see how the manufacturers made use of a few basic body styles to sell many different types of pedal cars. *Zone Five*

Zoom, zoom! Here I come! This Hot Rod Racer, with Nicholas Hamrick at the wheel, was produced in 1956 by Garton. The body style continued production into the 1960s. It featured yellow paint with red-and- black trim, a plated radiator ornament and hubcaps, chain drive, and artillery wheels.

New models were rolled out, and many existing offerings got new paint jobs, decals, and trim parts. Accessories, like working lights and sirens, made more of a comeback. There were pedal cars inspired by popular television shows of the day, such as *Dragnet* and *Roy Rogers*. A little competition seems to have done wonders in encouraging pedal car manufacturers to spruce up their offerings.

AMF added new models and improved existing designs once they purchased BMC.

The short-lived Speed-o-matic chain drive attempted to combine the pedal and chain drive into one unit. Speed-o-matic consisted of a pair of pedals that transferred power to the rear of the pedal car by long rods, like pedal drive. The rods, however, were attached to a sprocket that transferred power by way of a chain to another sprocket on the rear axle. With this system, which was discontinued by 1957, the driver had the back-and-forth action of pedal drive and the benefit of the gear ratio of chain

SPECIFICATIONS

Finished in Real Fire Engine
Red and Equipped with
Clang Bell and Two Lad-
ders. This Job Is Ready t
Take Off to a Fire at
Moment's Notice.

Body: Entire body made from
ne piece of steel.

Dimensions: Length: 45½"—
idth: 17½".

Material: Heavy gauge steel
ed in one-piece body and
ndergear.

Bumper and Grille: Bright sil-
r painted—Separate stamp-
g.

Steering Wheel: New modern
sign in white baked enamel
Metallic Pressure Sensitive
bel in center.

Drive Mechanism: Pedal drive
Adjustable ball bearing pull
aps.

Pedals: Solid rubber.

Wheels: 8" double disc in
hite enamel.

Hub Caps: Bright nickel plate
modern design.

Tires: ¾" extruded rubber.

Finish: Fire engine red baked
namel—Windshield finished
white baked enamel.

Trim: Attractive decorations
on side and hood—Loud
clanging bell—Two yellow
ladders on hangers finished
in white baked enamel —
Large V decal on rear.

Packing: One per carton.

Shipping Weight: 29 lbs.

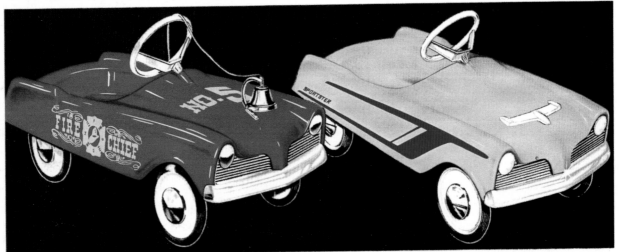

FIRE CHIEF STOCK NO. 82-1

These Items Spell More Profits and Sales for You. New in

Body: Entire body made from one piece of steel.

Dimensions: Length 38"—Width 17½".

Material: Heavy gauge steel used in one-piece body and undergear.

Bumper and Grille: Bright silver painted — Separate stamping.

Steering Wheel: New modern design in white baked enamel —Metallic Pressure Sensitive label in center.

Drive Mechanism: Pedal drive — Adjustable ball bearing pull straps.

Pedals: Solid rubber.

Wheels: 8" double disc in white baked enamel.

Hub Caps: Bright nickel plate in modern design.

Tires: ¾" extruded rubber.

Finish: Red baked enamel.

Trim: Attractive decorations on side and hood—Loud clang-ing bell—Large V decal on rear.

Packing: One per carton.

Shipping Weight: 26 lbs.

SPORTSTER STOCK NO. 81-1

design—Attractively finished—Modern decoration—Low in price.

Body: Entire body made from one piece of steel.

Dimensions: Length 38"—Width 17½".

Material: Heavy gauge steel used in one-piece body and undergear.

Bumper and Grille: Bright silver painted — Separate stamping.

Steering Wheel: New modern design in white baked enamel —Metallic Pressure Sensitive label in center.

Drive Mechanism: Pedal drive—Adjustable ball bearing pull straps.

Pedals: Solid rubber.

Wheels: 8" double disc in white baked enamel.

Hub Caps: Bright nickel plate in modern design.

Tires: ¾" extruded rubber.

Finish: Blue baked enamel.

Trim: Attractive decorations on side—Hood ornament fin-nished in white baked enamel—Large V decal on rear.

Packing: One per carton.

Three of the models from Midwest Industries. This page from the 1957 catalog shows what most people refer to as the 1953 Studebaker.

drive. There was even a two-speed version, with high and low gears that could be selected by way of a lever in the cockpit.

The body styles offered by AMF continued some models introduced by BMC, like the Jet series, which was offered as the Jet Liner, the Super Jet, and a Jet Liner Hook and Ladder, with a metal extension fitted on the back of the car body that held a pair of ladders and handrails. The Mainliner series of pedal cars and trucks featured the more conventional pedal drive and was available as a convertible, called the Pacesetter, a fire chief's car, a hook and ladder fire engine, and a dump truck. AMF also continued to offer pedal tractors to junior farmers everywhere.

The AMF Sportliner series featured more squared-off styling accented by a flat front-end treatment that did away with the heavy front bumper and grille treatments. It featured inset headlights, a finer egg-crate grille, and slightly raised hood that gave the cars the look of sports cars of the period. There was a convertible called the Supersport, a station

wagon, and a hook and ladder truck. All were powered by Speed-o-matic drive.

The Sportliner body style would be switched over to the Jet Liner name in 1956, and a host of fine pedal cars were offered. There was the Capri, with two Speed-o-matic drive, two-tone green-and-white finish, and battery-powered headlights and horn. This fine pedal car also had a continental-styled rear-mounted spare tire, twin chrome exhaust tips at the back bumper, and bullet-styled rear taillights. The Super Jet and Supersport convertibles were produced with the Speed-o-matic drive, while pedal drive was still offered on the Mainliner hook and ladder and the Jet Ace convertible.

Garton Manufacturing offered its Mark V and Mark XX designs, with lips over the recessed headlights, a raised hood, and heavy front bumper trim. The Mark V was the simpler of the two designs. It was powered by pedal drive and finished in green with white trim. It also offered a fire chief's car, finished in red with white trim, complete with a fire bell.

The Murray Champion, also referred to as the Dip Side Champion because of the way the rear fenders dip down. It was made between 1949 and 1959, and came in standard or deluxe models with different colors and graphic variations. It also came in a fire chief or fire truck body style. It was very popular then and today will demand between $1,200 and $1,500 in restored condition.

Made from 1955 to 1963, this Super Sonic Jet by Murray was 45 inches long with a wing spread of 25 inches. It had a chain drive, realistic dual jet controls, simulated gauges and instruments, a gear shift with realistic motor tone, and was painted in stratosphere blue with rocket red trim. One of Murray's nicest pedal toys, it was also available as the Sky Rocket or the Atomic Missile in different color combinations. *Zone Five*

There was also a hook and ladder truck, which featured a steel extension attached to the back of the car body. It was finished in red and came equipped with a pair of ladders and fire bell. The ranch wagon featured the same steel extension, but it was put to use as a station wagon. It had a two-tone blue-and-black finish and came with battery-powered headlights.

Finding inspiration in the popular *Dragnet* television series, the Dragnet auto was built off the Mark V design. Here are "just the facts" about the Dragnet car. It was white with black trim, powered by pedal drive and came with battery-powered microphone and loudspeaker. The Mark XX had the same

the all new "59" HAMILTON *Kiddybird*

No. 902

dream of the junior set

NO. 902 KIDDYBIRD

The new 1959 Kiddybird design and style is indeed the dream of every youngster. "Just like dad's new car!" The sculptured all plastic body is securely mounted on a rugged all steel channel constructed frame. Chain drive and easy steering for top performance. Packed one to carton. Shipping wt. 43 lbs.

SPECIFICATIONS
- All plastic body
- Steel channel constructed frame
- Wheels 1¼" x 8"
- Semi-pneumatic auto-type tires
- Chain drive and easy steering
- 50" long — 21" wide — 43 lbs.
- Trade marked

Rear view of the beautiful "59" Kiddybird. Outstanding styling in colorful plastic.

HAMILTON STEEL PRODUCTS, INC.
1845 WEST 74TH STREET • CHICAGO 36, ILLINOIS

body design as the Mark V, but was dressed up with a green-and-white two-tone finish and was powered by pedal drive.

The Kidillac was offered in two designs. Both versions were powered by chain drive and came with spare tires mounted on the rear bumper, driver's side mirror, aerial, and two-tone finishes. The base version was painted black and brown, while the more detailed model had a maroon-and-cream finish and battery-powered, working headlights.

AMF produced a series of heavy-duty trucks that were styled after the work trucks produced by GMC. The transport truck, with hinged rear gate, was finished in gold. The wrecker, equipped with a hand-cranked hoist and battery-powered flashing light, was finished in white with black trim. The hook and ladder, finished in red with yellow-and-white trim, had a fire bell, battery-powered flashing light and pair of ladders. All were powered by pedal drive.

Murray continued to offer many of the models they had introduced earlier in the decade, including the "Sad Face" series of trucks, the Champion, which was now the straight-sided version. The Champion body style was also put into service as the Ranchero. The three-wheeled motorcycles were now put into service as police and fire department vehicles.

For 1957, AMF decided fins were in, and its new "years ahead" design was inspired by Ford. The company did a fine job of capturing the look with dual headlights, heavy front bumper, and tailfins. This new design featured a trunk, so young drivers could travel with their luggage. Several models were offered, including a convertible, a fire chief's car, and a station wagon. There were also deluxe models available with battery-powered headlights. They also revised the front end look of their Jet Liner series, though they dropped all series names from this year forward.

For the remaining years of the 1950s, AMF offered new models based on the designs they had already created. The Hydraulic

Hamilton also made plastic-model pedal cars such as this 1959 Chevrolet. There are not many of these around today, and a nice one could bring $1,500+.

Christmas morning for a happy little boy with his 1953 Studebaker by Midwest Industries of Cleveland, Ohio.

Weapons Carrier consisted of the GMC truck with U.S. Air Force trim and swivel-mounted gun on the rear of the truck. AMF also offered electric power on its electric truck and a tractor called the Electrotrac.

Garton also continued to refine its current offerings, including the Mark series, creating several new models. Some of the new models were equipped with electric lights, windshields, and tailfins. The Garton Kidillac continued to be offered, with and without electric lights. Garton also introduced an Army jeep at the end of the decade.

The 1950s had seen pedal car makers work to bring back some of the glamour to pedal cars. Battery-powered accessories, mirrors, two-tone finishes, and interior detailing made a comeback of sorts. By the end of the decade, however, they were again trimming back their offerings, slowing the pace of development, and beginning to do away with accessories like lights and horns. It was a fine revival, but it did not go on forever.

THE PERFECT TOY FOR PARENTS.
IT RECHARGES ITS OWN BATTERY.

The Poweride electric car is a parent's dream. Once you pay for it, you won't have to keep paying for it over and over again. Because this toy has its own rechargeable battery.

When it weakens, just plug it into any wall outlet just overnight to give your child seven more hours of fun.

Moving around and exploring his world is a thrill your child won't outgrow. And it's nice to know that from the time he's two till the time he's eight he'll be able to hop on his own car and go.

Because its most important parts are made from Allied Chemical's PLASKON® Nylon, Poweride will last that long.

But don't worry, he won't go too far.

Poweride only goes up to two miles an hour. Poweride. It's a small price to pay for the perfect toy.

Other models available: Poweride Super Cycle and Poweride Hot Foot Dragster.

POWERIDE™
Eldon Industries, Inc.

Chapter Six

THE 1960s: THE FUTURE IS (SADLY) IN PLASTICS

The 1960s was a decade of change for pedal car manufacturers. The tailfin and chrome craze had died out rather quickly after the outrageous heights reached by 1959. The automotive styles of the early 1960s were more understated, as the excess and the chrome were reined back in. There were new models by all the auto makers, and the three largest pedal car manufacturers, AMF, Murray, and Garton, were still in rather fierce competition to offer the latest, most appealing designs they could produce.

In that sense, it seemed like little had changed in the world of pedal cars. There were still multiple manufacturers copying the most recent designs of the automotive world, but there were changes ahead that would ultimately spell the end for the pedal car as a standard of the toy business. Indeed, the 1960s was the last decade that manufacturers produced large numbers of steel-bodied pedal cars.

Murray Ohio produced a new model for 1960 that captured the new, more restrained styling very well. Murray's Tee Bird Auto, which had only the slightest resemblance to Ford's Thunderbird, did a credible job of capturing the new automotive subtlety. The Tee Bird was available as a passenger car, fire chief, and, with a pair of ladders mounted on the back, a fire

The Murray Company sold its pedal cars under the name Steelcraft beginning in 1924. Except for the years during World War II, manufacturing continued uninterrupted until 1973 when production ceased.

Plastic pedal or electric cars today are still popular with little kids, but the older metal-bodied cars are the ones that big kids are wanting.

which came complete with decals that simulated wood-grain paneling.

The tried-and-true Murray three-wheeler was kept in service as an Airport Service Truck and the Atomic Missile was still offered. Murray's Super Deluxe pedal tractor took authenticity to a new level by adding spark plug wires to the sides of the "engine" for added realism. For several years to come, the big three pedal car makers turned their attention to providing realistic-looking engines to many of their pedal car creations.

For the Garton Toy Company of Wisconsin, the early 1960s saw one of its best sellers reach the end of its road. The Garton Kidillac, which had so faithfully captured the tailfin-inspired designs of the 1950s was on its way out. The Kidillac, still offered as late as 1961, was available in both deluxe and standard models. The chain-drive deluxe Kidillac was the finer of the two, complete with continental spare tire and battery-powered headlights.

These two photographs show Don Little, his brother Steve, and father James, on Christmas morning 1960 in Charlotte, North Carolina. The 1960 fire chief car by Murray was finished in scarlet red with white trim. This model also came as a fire truck, and the popular Thunderbird. The T-Bird model came in balawa blue with white trim. All of these models were referred to as V-nose models, because of the shape of the grille. The Western Flyer tractor also by Murray was a super deluxe model with chain drive, simulated spark plugs and ignition wires, motor-tone gear shift, a trailer hitch, and a spring-adjustable seat. This model came in red, green, or yellow.

truck. Known today as the V face, this basic Murray design served the company well for many years.

The other big seller in the Murray line-up in the early 1960s was the model based on the 1959 Ford, which was the first of the big three auto makers to tone down its styling.

Introduced in 1959, this new Murray design saw service as everything from a speedway pace car to a station wagon. The wagon design featured a steel extension of the rear fenders and was used to create a circus wagon, fire truck, dump truck with working bed, and the station wagon deluxe,

Garton did have new offerings, including the Casey Jones locomotive, which was a tribute to the great steam locomotives of the past. Powered by pedal drive, the Casey Jones was equipped with smoke stack, cow catcher, and a nonworking headlight. The "coal tender" two-wheeled cart could be ordered separately to complete the train look.

Garton's Hot Rod, which had been available since the 1950s, received a makeover that added new styling touches, including a windshield. It was powered by pedal drive.

The Mark V series of Garton cars also continued to be offered as a simple passenger car, a fire chief's car, and a fire "truck" that was simply the car design with two ladders mounted on brackets to the rear fenders. The jeep model introduced in the late 1950s saw service as an Air Force jeep and a fire truck equipped with a pair of ladders. Later Army versions came well-armed with a bazooka mounted on the driver's side and a camouflage version with a machine gun mounted on the hood.

AMF started the 1960s off with tried-and-true models like the star-grilled model 514 "customized" pedal car. One of the most-decal laden models ever offered, the 514 had an extensive set of decals that could be ap-plied as the owner saw fit. Powered by pedal drive, the "custom" also featured hubcaps with the AMF-embossed jeweled reflector. The same body style was offered as several different models including a fire chief

On the right is an original National pedal scooter called the Super Rider. On the left is a one-of-a-kind custom Indian pedal-motorcycle/sidecar combo created by co-author Ed Weirick.

The Murray Super Sport, Comet, and Torpedo all used the same body style, but had different colors and graphic designs. The Super Sport would be the rarest to find in a good to excellent original condition today. Any of these models will bring $2,500+ today in restored condition.

with bell and ladders, the Skylark with continental-styled rear end, hood ornament, and metallic green finish, and the more basic Jet Sweep. All were powered by pedal drive and rode on solid disc wheels.

When the go-kart arrived in the late 1950s, older children had one-up on their younger siblings and their pedal cars. With its simple tube frame and small gas engine, the go-kart provided the most realistic driving experience yet, and it found great success with older children. Pedal car makers were quick to offer younger riders, who were not quite ready for such a complete driving experience, a more tame pedal version.

AMF's Scat Car made its debut in 1960, and perfectly captured the look of the go-kart. The basic frame of steel tubing with a simple seat was the go-kart to a tee. It even had a metal plate behind the rear seat that was covered by a large decal of a small gas engine for added realism. By 1962 the Scat Car was available in three versions, two with chain drive, the other with pedal drive.

From the late 1950s into the mid-1960s this AMF model was most recognized as the Pacesetter. It also came out as a fire chief car, the Skylark, the Jet Sweep, a fire department hook and ladder, the Custom 514, a dump truck, and a highway patrol car. Many pedal car collectors and restorers like to customize these cars to their own liking. *Zone Five*

This Tin Lizzie was made from the early 1960s until 1968 by Garton Co. This cute car looked like a vintage 1920s or 1930s vehicle. Garton used the body for other models. The hood ornament was originally used on an earlier model, and Garton decided to use it again on the 1960s version to give it that extra touch. A restored or nice original would bring $1,500+. *Zone Five*

Murray also joined in the go-kart craze with its Tot Rod, powered by pedal drive, and the Super Tot Rod, powered by chain drive. By 1963, Murray added a basic body, side exhaust, and race car decals to the regular Tot Rod design and created the Fire Ball and Thunderbolt racers. The Fire Ball featured an adjustable seat and chain drive, while the Thunderbolt was powered by pedal drive

Garton, which often followed the lead of AMF and Murray, created its Hawk pedal cart to match the latest inspiration of the pedal car world. The Hawk was produced in two versions: The more basic model was powered by pedal drive, while the chain drive Hawk featured a stylized nose and tail.

It was 1964 when America was presented with a new concept in automobiles, the Ford Mustang. Championed by a young Lee Iococca, the Mustang was a sporty two-door that

featured a new long-nose, short-trunk body style that looked terrific and did a fine job of hiding the Mustang's kinship to Ford's economical, rather plain Falcon compact car. In a breakthrough in the pedal car world, AMF

A 1961 Hot Rod by Garton. This is the same body style as one often seen in yellow, and this body was also used for the Tin Lizzie, Casey Jones, and other models from the late 1940s to the late 1960s. *Zone Five*

The red car is a Champion by Murray and the blue car is a 1961 Murray T-Bird.

actually teamed up with Ford to produce a pedal version of the Mustang.

Finished in red, and powered by pedal drive, the AMF Mustang was first available at Ford dealerships in time for Christmas in 1964. The price for the pedal pony car was a more than reasonable $12.95. The following year, the Mustang was sold by AMF at traditional retail outlets like toy and department stores. Like most of the pedal cars from this era, the Mustang featured a steel body, with trim parts made of plastic. It was subtly refined several times during its life and would continue to be produced for many years, with production finally ending in 1972.

The rest of the AMF line-up for the mid-1960s featured pedal cars that had more ornamentation than anything seen in quite some time. The Suburbanite, Super Sport, and Skylark featured clear plastic windshields, chrome luggage racks, continental-styled spare tires, bulb horns, side mirrors, built-in storage compartments, plated gearshifts, and plenty of decals to dress them up.

The AMF Junior Dragster, first offered in 1965, was inspired by America's growing fascination with drag racing. Sharing common construction with the Scat Cars, the Dragster was available in king and regular sizes. Both featured a simulated V-8 mounted in front of the driver and a chrome rollbar. Both versions were powered by chain drive.

AMF really increased the detail and selection of their pedal tractors in the mid-1960s, including several models that featured simulated engines that could be seen under the hood. The Big 4, Power Trac, Super Trac, and Ranch Trac were powered by chain drive and featured simulated engines. The Super Trac was the largest of the group, measuring 42 inches long and 24 inches wide. The Ranch Trac was available with an optional noisemaker that created engine sound. There were also accessories offered, like an umbrella and a two-wheeled cart.

The Big 4, Ranch Trac, and Super Trac also featured a new front-end design that moved the front wheels apart in a more car-like fashion. The new design was said to add stability and require less effort in turning. The drive to come up with the most realistic engine prompted AMF to offer its battery-powered "Action Motor," which featured a moving valvetrain and turning radiator fan.

For the mid-1960s Garton decided to turn back the clock when it offered its Tin Lizzie, a tribute of Henry Ford's Model T,

This super advertisement from 1964 shows the Kidillac by Garton, made from 1950 to 1960. It came in a standard and deluxe model.

INTRODUCING THE DEPENDABLES FOR '64

We didn't invent the compact . . .

we just enlarged upon it!

The original idea about compacts has little similarity to the 1964 Dart idea. Now don't get us wrong. Dart certainly is a compact. It parks almost anywhere. It steers quickly, handles lightly. It's about as easy on gas as you hope to get. But from there on out the old idea and the new part company . . . Because Dart's the compact in the large economy size! Dart looks bigger. It sits bigger.

It's powered bigger. And the Dart trunk is actually larger than many standard-size cars. When you add it all up, here's a lot of car going for you. A lot of room and comfort. A lot of durability and service-saving features. A lot of good looks that take you out of the compact class without taking you away from a compact price. The 1964 Dodge Dart! America's new family-size favorite.

Compact Dodge Dart

DODGE DIVISION ✦ CHRYSLER MOTORS CORPORATION

From 1959 to the late 1960s this body style by Murray was often referred to as the 1959 Ford. It was also released as the Astronaut's Car, the Radio Sports Car, a pace car, fire chief car, the Thunder Jet, the Dude Wagon, and still more. This car is still very popular today because of its appeal to baby boomers and their childhood memories. *Zone Five*

which had helped get America on wheels after the turn of the century. Basically a Garton Hot Rod with fenders, headlamps, and a windshield, the Tin Lizzie later came equipped with a canvas roof.

With the emphasis on adding realistic-looking and sounding engines to pedal cars, Garton's Sonda attempted to combine the realistic motor and the mid-1960s popularity of minibikes and scooters. One consonant away from being a Honda, the Sonda was a scooter design that featured full-sized wheels on the front and rear, plus a pair of training wheels on the back for added stability. The Sonda was available in two models, one featured the noise-making motor and one did not.

Other Garton offerings including the pedal-powered GT series of cars, which seemed to take their styling from British sports cars of the period. The Garton tractor efforts also emphasized the realistic engine look, with models that featured the exposed

A 1960 pedal motorcycle by the Mobo Co. of England. There are not many of these around and they are highly desirable. The value would be in the $1,000+ range.

"Oh, but officer . . ." The 1965 AMF Mustang and the 1956 Garton Police Department pedal cars, driven by Amanda Poulin and Eric Folmer are both restored.

The Garton Spin-A-Roo was made between 1963 to 1966. Its value today is about $500. *Zone Five*

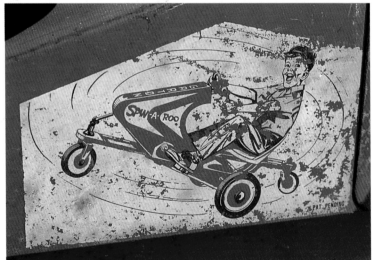

spark plug wires and a version that had the same motor as the Sonda under the hood.

For all the efforts that pedal car makers seemed to put into creating more realistic-looking engines, body styles remained relatively unchanged. Gone were the days when new tooling would create completely new pedal cars every three to four years. Instead, decals and plastic trim parts, far less

expensive to change than dies, were used to create different models.

Much of the detail and authenticity seemed to be slipping away from the pedal car world after the mid-1960s. There were "fire trucks" produced by all three manufacturers that were nothing more than basic car bodies with a pair of ladders mounted on the rear fenders. In 1968, Murray, which had often led the field in terms of producing realistic pedal cars, was still offering body styles that had debuted in 1959. They were now nine years old, and their age showed. They continued to be offered, regardless of their age, through 1972.

Murray, however, did have a new set of pedal vehicles that were unlike anything seen before. The Murray Jolly Roger, Skipper, and Dolphin Gulf Stream were three-wheeled, pedal-powered pleasure boats that looked like child-sized versions of the real thing. The Skipper and Jolly Roger were available with optional outboard motors and chrome bow rails. Murray also offered a new body style of car called the Charger, which took its name

from Dodge's sporty two-door. The Charger was available as a passenger car, fire chief's car, and with the addition of two ladders on rear fenders, a fire truck.

It was 1969 when one of the big three pedal car makers finally turned its attention to plastic bodies. Though there had been other pedal car manufacturers that offered plastic bodies, including the Irwin Company, which produced the *Flintstones* car among others, AMF, Murray, and Garton stuck with steel construction through 1968. The Garton Toy Company changed all that in 1969, when it offered five different pedal cars with plastic bodies. All had steel frames and were powered by pedal drive.

All the Garton plastic-bodied pedal cars, which were made from "tough injection-molded Polypropylene" seemed to have a

The pedal car was used in many advertisements, such as this one for LP gas. Here we see a Murray of Ohio, whose body style was used for fire chief cars, pace cars, and many other types from 1959 to the late 1960s.

Will LP-gas make my car go, Mister?

If your car had an engine, son, LP-gas would make it go lickety-split.

LP-gas makes my truck go, just as it runs buses, tractors, and taxis.

And many of the trucks you see on the highway are powered by LP-gas just like gasoline or diesel fuel.

But engine fuel is only one of the hundreds of ways LP-gas is used.

IT HEATS HOMES, DRIES CLOTHES, IRRIGATES FIELDS, CURES TOBACCO.

In fact, of America's great sources of energy, only LP-gas serves you in so many ways.

People in towns, suburbs and on farms use LP-gas just as people served by utilities use natural gas.

Wherever heat and power are required, LP-gas does the job.

These are some of the reasons why over 11 million families use LP-gas.

Of America's great sources of energy, only LP-gas serves you in so many ways.

LP-GAS FOR COOKING
LP-GAS FOR AIR CONDITIONING
LP-GAS FOR FLAME WEEDING
LP-GAS FOR HOME HEATING

NATIONAL LP-GAS MARKET DEVELOPMENT COUNCIL,
Chicago, Illinois 60603

The Big 4 Tractor by AMF was made in several combinations from the mid 1960s to early 1970s. Made of heavy gauge steel with realistic action motor, chain drive, spring mounted adjustable seat, and a trailer hitch. *Zone Five*

British influence. There were three open-wheeled race cars, which took their styling from Formula One competitors like Lotus. The Sprite, Deluxe Sprite, and Formula II racer were all single-seaters that shared the same body design. The Sprite was the simplest of the three, followed by the Deluxe Sprite, which had plastic side exhaust, while the Formula II had a plastic rear-mounted engine.

The other plastic offerings were the GT, which had opening doors, hood, and trunk. The hood was referred to as the "bonnet," and the trunk was called the "boot," furthering the British influences in the advertising copy. The hood, or bonnet if you are so inclined, opened to reveal a simulated engine. The final plastic bodied pedal car was the Chubby. Its rounded body and decals that made the headlights look like eyes gave it a cartoon-like appearance.

Let's Race

2 $15⁸⁸

1 5-MPH ELECTRIC $49⁸⁸ cash without battery NO MONEY DOWN

3 $13⁹⁹

4 $13⁸⁸

5 $8⁸⁸

1 **Electric-drive Kart.** All you do is drive . . the battery does the work. Push gear stick up for forward, down for reverse or let it idle in neutral. Holds road when cornering . . won't exceed 5 mph. Pull hand-brake to stop. Automobile-type link steering. Tubular steel frame. Plastic foam seat, 8-inch wheels with 1¾-inch knobby-tread tires. Red with silver trim. Uses 12-volt storage battery, order below. To keep battery power up to capacity, order 12-volt battery booster 28 G 7169 from Sears General Catalog. Kart and battery shipped freight (rail or truck) or express.
79 N 8977N—46x27½ inches wide over-all. Helmet not included Shpg. wt. 45 lbs. $49.88
28 N 13N—12-volt battery. Shpg. wt. 47 pounds. 18.95

2 **Chain-drive Tot Rod.** The smaller set will be rarin' to pedal places on this sleek job! Jet-style steering wheel makes it a snap to handle. Rolls smoothly on 10-inch rear wheels, 8-inch ball-bearing front wheels . . all rubber tires. Sturdy tubular steel wedge frame with comfortable bucket seat. Rubber-covered roll bar. Fire-engine red with striking white trim. 41x23 inches wide over-all.
79 N 8976L—Shipping weight 30 pounds. $15.88

3 **Pedal-drive Scat Car.** 4 ft. long, almost 2 ft. (23 in.) wide! Smooth ball-bearing drive . . pedals adjust to 5 positions. ¾-in. tubular steel frame. 10-in. rear, 7-in. front wheels; 1¾-in. tires. Footrests extend for coasting. Raised seat, roll-over bar. Red with black and white trim. Shpg. wt. 27 lbs.
79 N 8019L. $13.99

4 **Push-type Racer.** Rugged "track-burner" has aluminum-finish steel frame, reinforced axles. 8-in. graphite-bearing wheels, 1¾-in. tires. Foot or hand brake, steering wheel. Plywood seat, Masonite Presdwood back. 53x 18 in. wide. Wt. 22 lbs.
79 N 8965L. $13.88

5 **Push-type Tot's Racer.** Low, road-hugging design prevents tipping on the turns. Oversize, non-mar plastic wheels—7-in. diameter in rear, 5-in. front—add stability. Steel frame. Auto-type steering wheel. Adjustable footrests. Simulated motor. Masonite Presdwood seat and back. 42x18 in. wide.
79N8018C—Wt. 10 lbs.$8.88

Air Force Jeep

Carry out important missions with chain-drive ease. Ball-bearing pedal crank and rear axle supports. Windshield raises or lowers. 8-inch nylon-bearing wheels, treaded semi-pneumatic tires. Steel body. Auto-type steering. Blue with yellow trim. 41¾ inches long. Easy to assemble. Shipping weight 38 pounds.
79 N 8978L. $18.88

$18⁸⁸

NOTE: All cars on these 2 pages are partly assembled . . easy to set up

USAF 82412

Tee Bird Auto

$9⁶⁶

Hop in and give it a spin . . here's freewheeling fun! Ball-bearing pull straps and axle hangers make pedaling smooth and easy. Adjustable pedals. 8-in. double-disc wheels with molded rubber tires. Jet-type steering wheel. Sturdy body. Blue with trim, red wheels, white trim. 3 long. Easy t Shipping 79 N 8

386 SEARS 3 PCS

This ad from a 1960s Sears catalog shows some of the pedal vehicles then available. Reflecting a big fad of the 1960s, they look more like go-carts than cars.

An AMF 1967 GTO—done up with custom paint. This model had a plated gearshift, spinner hub caps, embossed silver headlights, and bumpers. This body style was also used for the Suburbanite, a fire chief car, and the Super Sport. *Zone Five*

While the benefits of plastic included lighter weight, resistance to rust, and greater safety for the rider, the introduction of molded plastic bodies helped usher out the days of the steel-bodied pedal cars. By 1971 AMF had joined the ranks of the plastic-bodied cars with its dune buggy. AMF held out a few more years, bringing out its plastic-bodied fire truck in the mid-1970s.

Not all was lost in the pedal car world after the introduction of plastic bodies. The muscle car craze of the late 1960s, which produced some very sporty, powerful youth-oriented machines, inspired some pedal cars as well. The GTO and GTX by AMF found their inspiration in the Pontiac and the Plymouth that they were named after. The GTX was the more outrageous of the two, featuring a lime green finish, complete with large black rally stripes on the hood. Murray's Dragon Fire took things even further. The Dragon Fire was built on the Charger body and featured a large engine protruding out of the hood.

For all efforts put into the later steel-bodied pedal cars, it was only a matter of time before they faded away. By 1975, Garton, having undergone a reorganization a few years earlier, was out of the pedal car business for good. Murray, which carried on until 1973, quit pedal car production to turn its manufacturing efforts to more profitable items like children's bicycles. AMF continued on until the 1980s, finally selling off its plant in 1982.

The steel-bodied pedal cars left the scene quietly, their fate sealed by changing technologies and consumer tastes. The pedal cars grew up right beside the automobile, faithfully following the evolution of the car. In the end, that might have been the pedal car's greatest undoing, as automobiles became less unique and interesting, their individuality slipped away. Time wore down the public's fascination with their cars.

Simrex Models Inc. of Miweola, New York, made this Ford reproduction in the 1960s and 1970s. It was meant to resemble an early turn-of-the-century model. Even adults can drive this neat creation. *Zone Five*

Pedal cars were built of steel, and they more than stood the test of time. By following the trends of the automotive world, they reflect the grandeur, the whimsy, and the progress of the automobile. After finding their way into attics and basements, pedal cars have been reclaimed and rediscovered by collectors. Now they are displayed as proud symbols of a time that has passed.

This is the 1961 Casey Jones Locomotive from Garton. It was available with or without the coal tender. Two other models by Garton, the Hot Rod and the Tin Lizzie, used the same body. Its price today is in the $1,500 range. *Zone Five*

This cute little Volkswagen pedal car has a metal body with plastic trim and was available in red or yellow. It came out in the 1970s and is still available. It could also be purchased as an electric model. Retail today is between $150 and $200. *Zone Five*

RECOMMENDED READING

The 20th Century-Year by Year. Marshall Editions Ltd., 1998.

Dammann, George H. *Sixty Years of Chevrolet.* Sarasota, FL: Crestline Publishing Co., 1972.

Heydt, Read. *Urban Renewal To Replace Gendron Building.* Toledo Blade, August 10, 1967.

Gregano , G. N. *Cars 1886-1930.* New York: Beekman House, 1986.

Gurka, Andrew G. *Pedal Car Restoration and Price Guide.* Iola, WI: Krause Publications, 1996.

Lee, John. *Standard Catalog of Chrysler 1924-1990.* Iola, WI: Krause Publications, 1995.

Lichty, Robert. *Standard Catalog of Ford 1903-1990.* Iola, WI: Krause Publications, 1995.

Lucey, Charles T. *Gendron Wheel Co. Is Santa Claus to World.* Toledo Blade May 23, 1927.

Massucci, Edoardo. *Cars for Kids.* New York: Rizzoli International, 1983.

Pennell, Paul. *Children's Cars.* Shire Publications Ltd., 1986.

Porter, Tara Mosier. *Santa's Helpers.* Toledo Metropolitan December, 1986.

Sedgewick, Michael. *Cars of the Thirties and Forties.* New York: Beekman House, 1986.

Shaffer, Mark. *Gendron Celebrates 125th Anniversary.* Archibald (Ohio) Buckeye August 20, 1997.

Standard Catalog of Cadillac 1903-1990. Edited by Ken Buttolph, Mary Sieber: Iola, WI: Krause Publications, 1995.

Vivian, David. *Encyclopedia of American Cars,* New York, NY: Crescent Books, 1994.

Wood, Neil S. *Evolution of the Pedal Car-1884-1970s.* Gas City, IN: L-W Book Sales, 1989.

Wood, Neil S. *Evolution of the Pedal Car, Volume 2.* Gas City, IN: L-W Book Sales, 1990.

Wood, Neil S. *Evolution of the Pedal Car, Volume 3.* Gas City, IN: L-W Book Sales, 1992.

Wood, Neil S. *Evolution of the Pedal Car, Volume 4.* Gas City, IN: L-W Book Sales, 1993.

DETERMINING VALUES

The prices shown in this guide may vary somewhat for several reasons, including where or how the toy was obtained. Auctions, toy shows, private sales, flea markets, and antique shops are good sources. Also, prices sometimes fluctuate in different parts of the country. This value guide shows some of the many different makes and models that represent the more popular and familiar pre- and post-war pedal vehicles.

It isn't always how old the pedal vehicles are that determines their worth. The make, style, character, rarity, demand, and of course, availability and condition are important factors in determining value. While we have attempted to compile prices from several sources in many different regions, buyers should be aware that the prices in this book serve as a guide only. We recommend that any novice consult with experienced collectors and dealers before they purchase. Whether an excellent original or restored car, it's really up to the individual person to decide what he or she wants to pay.

CONDITIONS

Fair: Could be rusty, with small dents, a pitted finish, dirty and incomplete, but still a fairly good restorable model. Needs a complete restoration.

Good: Should be fairly complete and solid. May have light rust, some small dings. A good restorable model or could be left original and reconditioned as needed.

Excellent Original: Exceptionally complete, all original. Showing little or no wear, minute nicks and scratches.

Authentically Restored: A quality restoration, as close as possible and properly restored to the original. Using original parts when possible.

VALUES

Manufacturer	Model or Style	Year	Fair	Good	CONDITION Excellent Original	Authentically Restored
AMF	Thunderbolt	1956	250	400	$1,200	$900
AMF	Super Sport	1956	300	500	1,400	1,000
AMF	Hook & Ladder	1956	150	250	600	500
AMF	Fire Dept.	1959	125	225	550	450
AMF	Fire Chief	1959	100	200	500	400
AMF	Pacesetter	1959	100	200	500	400
AMF	Thunder Streak	1959	250	500	1,400	1,200
AMF	Cab over - Mail Truck	1959	500	800	1,600	1,500
AMF	Tow Wrecker	1959	400	600	1,400	1,200
AMF	Surburbanite	1960	250	500	1,400	1,200
AMF	Jet Sweep	1960	75	150	450	300
AMF	Super Sport	1965	150	250	600	500
AMF	Sky Lark	1965	100	250	800	600
AMF	Dragster	1965	75	150	500	350
AMF	Mustang	1965	200	400	1,200	900
AMF	Fire Fighter 508	1967	75	150	450	350
AMF	Jr. Trac	1967	75	125	350	250
AMF	Probe Jr.	1971	50	100	400	200
AMF	H & L Pumper	1971	75	150	450	350
AMF	Mustang	1971	200	400	1,000	800
AMF	GTO	1971	75	125	450	350
AMF	GTX	1971	75	125	450	350
AMF	Pacer	1977	60	100	400	300
AMERICAN NATIONAL	Cadillac	1920s	2,000	2,500	6,500	4,500
AM. NAT.	Stake Body Truck	1920s	3,500	4,500	9,000	6,000
AM. NAT.	Packard	1921	6,500	10,000	15,000	12,000
AM. NAT.	Paige	1925	2,500	4,000	6,500	5,000
AM. NAT.	Silver King	1927	3,000	4,500	8,000	6,000
AM. NAT.	Federal Dump	1927	5,000	6,500	12,000	8,500
AM. NAT.	Packard Coupe	1925	10,000	15,000	25,000	25,000
AM. NAT.	Overland	1933	1,000	1,500	3,000	2,500
AM. NAT.	Chevrolet	1933	1,200	1,600	3,500	2,800
AM. NAT.	Buick	1933	2,500	4,000	7,500	6,000
AM. NAT.	Auburn	1933	3,000	4,500	8,500	6,500
AM. NAT.	Lincoln	1933	3,000	4,500	8,500	6,500
AM. NAT.	Fire Dept.	1933	2,200	3,200	5,500	4,500
AM. NAT.	Air Flow	1935	3,500	5,000	12,000	7,500
AM. NAT	Air Pilot	1935	3,000	4,000	8,000	5,500
AM. NAT	Wasp	1935	2,500	3,000	5,000	4,000
AM. NAT.	Buick	1935	3.500	4,000	8,000	6,500
AM. NAT.	Cadillac	1935	4,000	5,000	9,000	7,000
AM. NAT.	La Salle	1935	3,500	4,000	8,000	6,500
AM. NAT.	Lincoln	1935	6,000	8,000	15,000	12,000
AM. NAT.	Packard	1935	4,500	5,500	10,000	8,000
AM. NAT.	Racer	1935	4,000	5,500	10,000	8,000
AM. NAT.	Tandem	1935	6,500	8,000	15,000	12,000
AM. NAT.	Highway Dump	1935	2,000	4,000	6,500	5,000
AM. NAT.	White Dump	1935	3,000	4,500	7,500	5,500
AM. NAT.	Pontiac	1935	2,000	3,000	5,500	4,500

Manufacturer	Model or Style	Year	Fair	Good	CONDITION Excellent Original	Authentically Restored
AUSTIN	Austin J 40	1949–1971	800	1,500	3,000	3,000
BMC	Racer	1951	350	800	1,500	1,500
BMC	Station Wagon	1951	200	350	800	650
BMC	Tractor Sr.	1951	150	300	600	600
BMC	Jet Liner	1952	200	350	800	650
BMC	Pacesetter	1953	200	350	800	650
BMC	Thunderbolt	1953	250	450	1,000	900
BMC	Tractor Jr.	1953	100	150	400	300
BMC	Deluxe Tractor	1953	125	175	500	400
BMC	Dump Truck	1953	200	350	900	750
BMC	Hook & Ladder	1954	150	300	700	600

Add From $100 to $500 for Attachments:
Such as Trailer, Scoop-Shovel, Grader, Dump Cart, Snow Plow, Fire Fighter, Wrecker, Sulky

Manufacturer	Model or Style	Year	Fair	Good	Excellent Original	Authentically Restored
ESKA	Corvette	1956	1,500	2,500	4,000	3,500
GARTON	Pierce-Arrow	1916	1,800	2,500	4,500	3,500
GARTON	Packard	1916	1,600	2,400	4,500	3,500
GARTON	Buick	1916	1,500	2,000	4,000	3,200
GARTON	Tractor	1916	600	1,000	2,000	1,500
GARTON	Racer	1917	2,000	2,500	5,000	4,500
GARTON	Buick	1927	2,500	3,000	6,000	5,000
GARTON	Cadillac	1927	2,500	3,000	6,000	5,000
GARTON	Pontiac	1930	1,500	2,000	4,000	3,500
GARTON	Reo	1930	1,200	1,600	3,000	2,500
GARTON	Curtiss Airplane	1930	2,000	2,800	6,500	5,000
GARTON	Hook & Ladder	1930	1,600	2,000	5,000	4,500
GARTON	Chrysler	1933	2,000	2,500	5,000	4,500
GARTON	Pontiac	1935	1,500	2,000	4,000	3,500
GARTON	Oldsmobile	1937	1,500	2,000	4,000	3,500
GARTON	Ford	1938	1,800	2,500	5,000	4,000
GARTON	Lincoln	1938	2,000	2,800	5,500	4,500
GARTON	Divebomber Airplane	1941	5,000	6,500	10,000	8,000
GARTON	Army Tank	1941	3,000	5,000	8,500	7,000
GARTON	Station Wagon	1941	1,500	2,000	3,500	3,000
GARTON	Kidillac	1950–1960	600	1,000	2,500	2,000
GARTON	Fire Truck	1949	150	300	1,000	800
GARTON	Space Cruiser	1953	1,000	1,500	2,500	2,200
GARTON	Dragnet	1956	200	600	2,000	1,500
GARTON	Mark V	1956	200	400	1,000	800
GARTON	Hot Rod	1956	400	700	2,000	1,800
GARTON	Ranch Wagon	1959	150	400	1,000	800
GARTON	Tin Lizzie	1961	200	400	1,200	1,000
GARTON	Casey Jones Locomotive	1961	300	500	1,600	1,200
GENDRON	Champion	1906	1,500	2,500	5,000	5,000
GENDRON	Racer	1915	1,800	2,500	6,000	5,000
GENDRON	Packard	1915	2,000	3,000	6,500	5,500
GENDRON	Buick	1916	2,000	3,000	6,500	5,500
GENDRON	Locomotive	1916	2,000	3,000	6,000	5,000
GENDRON	Hook & Ladder	1924	2,000	3,000	5,500	4,500
GENDRON	Racer	1922	3,000	5,000	8,000	7,500
GENDRON	Hook & Ladder	1924	3,000	4,000	8,500	7,500

Manufacturer	Model or Style	Year	Fair	Good	Excellent Original	Authentically Restored
GENDRON	Dump Truck	1927	3,000	4,000	8,000	7,000
GENDRON	Jordan	1929	3,000	4,000	7,500	6,500
GENDRON	Race Car	1932	3,000	4,500	8,000	8,000
GENDRON	Ladder Truck	1935	1,500	2,200	3,500	3,500
GENDRON	Fire Chief	1936	800	1,200	2,200	1,800
GENDRON	Aeroplane	1938	2,000	3,000	6,500	5,500
GENDRON	Skippy Fire Dept.	1938	1,600	2,400	3,500	3,500
GENDRON	Skippy Roadster	1938	2,000	2,500	5,500	4,000
GENDRON	Skippy Racer	1938	4,000	5,000	10,000	9,000
GENDRON	Dump Truck	1938	1,500	2,500	5,000	4,000
GENDRON	Hose Cart	1938	4,000	5,000	9,000	7,500
GENDRON	Pioneer Roadster	1938	2,000	2,500	5,500	4,000
GENDRON	Pioneer Locomotive	1938	4,500	5,500	10,000	8,500
GENDRON	Air King	1938	3,000	4,500	8,500	6,000
GENDRON	Skippy Roadster	1940	2,500	4,000	6,500	5,000
GENDRON	Skippy Racer	1940	4,000	5,000	10,000	9,000
GIORDANI	Race Car	1955	2,000	3,000	5,500	5,500
GIORDANI	Woody Wagon	1950s	800	1,000	2,000	2,000
GIORDANI	Studebaker Bullet Nose	1950s	4,000	6,000	10,000	10,000
GIORDANI	Tandem	1920s	4,500	6,500	12,000	12,000
GIORDANI	Race Car - Boat Tail	1930s	5,000	6,000	12,000	12,000
GIORDANI	Spider	1920s	3,000	5,000	8,000	8,000
GIORDANI	Micky Mouse Car	1969	75	250	650	400
HAMILTON	Nellybelle	1954	500	800	1,500	1,500
HAMILTON	Jeep Army	1955	150	350	800	700
HAMILTON	Jeep Air Force	1955	150	350	800	700
HAMILTON	Jeep Tow Truck	1958	250	500	1,200	1,000
HAMILTON	Jeep Fire Truck	1958	150	350	700	600
HAMILTON	Chevrolet Fiber Glass	1958	300	600	2,000	2,000
KIRK-LATTY MFG.	Star	1914	1,400	2,000	4,000	3,200
KIRK-LATTY MFG.	Buick	1915	1,800	2,400	4,500	3,500
KIRK-LATTY MFG.	Cadillac	1914	1,800	2,800	4,500	4,000
KIRK-LATTY MFG.	Winton	1913	2,500	3,500	5,000	5,000
MIDWEST IND.	Tractor	1953	50	150	500	450
MIDWEST IND.	Sportster	1953	250	450	1,200	1,000
MIDWEST IND.	Fire Chief	1954	200	400	1,000	900
MIDWEST IND.	City Fire Dept.	1954	200	450	1,200	1,000
MIDWEST IND.	Jet Hawk	1957	300	500	1,400	1,200
MOBO	Motorcycle	1960s	250	450	1,000	1,000
MOBO	Horse	1939–50s	150	300	650	500
MOBO	Sm. Sulky-Slotted Wheels	1940s–50s	150	250	500	500
MOBO	Med. Sulky-Spoke Wheels	1940s–50s	200	300	600	600
MOBO	Lg. Sulky-Spoke Wheels	1940s–50s	200	350	800	800
MURRAY	Pontiac	1948	600	800	1,500	1,500
MURRAY	U.S. Pursuit Plane	1949–50	1,200	2,000	3,500+	3,500+
MURRAY	Pontiac Station Wagon	1948	350	700	1,200	1,200
MURRAY	Comet	1949	600	1,500	2,500	2,500
MURRAY	Fire Chief	1949	500	800	1,400	1,300

Manufacturer	Model or Style	Year	Fair	Good	CONDITION Excellent Original	Authentically Restored
MURRAY	City Fire Dept.	1950	600	1,000	1,500	1,500
MURRAY	Torpedo	1950	800	1,500	3,000	2,500
MURRAY	Champion (Dip Side)	1950–59	300	600	1,500	1,500
MURRAY	Champion (Slab Side)	1954	200	300	900	800
MURRAY	Ranch Wagon - Sad Face	1952	350	750	1,200	1,200
MURRAY	Sad Face Dump	1954	350	800	1,500	1,500
MURRAY	Trac Tractor (extra for trailer)	1952	100	350	800	700
MURRAY	Champion Royal Deluxe	1955	350	550	1,600	1,600
MURRAY	Super Sonic jet	1955	600	1,000	1,800	1,600
MURRAY	Police Cycle	1955	350	750	1,400	1,200
MURRAY	Good Humor truck	1955	400	800	1,500	1,500
MURRAY	Lancer	1956	600	750	1,200	1,200
MURRAY	Atomic Missile	1958	600	1,000	1,800	1,600
MURRAY	Super Deluxe Fire Truck	1959	600	750	1,200	1,200
MURRAY	Deluxe Station Wagon	1959	350	700	1,200	1,200
MURRAY	Pace Car	1961	150	400	1,000	800
MURRAY	Circus Wagon	1961	150	400	1,000	850
MURRAY	Tot Rod	1961	50	150	350	350
MURRAY	T Bird Auto	1961	150	250	500	500
MURRAY	Earth Mover	1962	250	425	1,150	1,000
MURRAY	Tractor	1963	75	150	400	400
MURRAY	Fire Ball Racer	1963	100	200	400	350
MURRAY	Charger Auto	1968	60	125	400	350
MURRAY	Fire Truck	1968	75	150	500	450
MURRAY	Jolly Roger Flag Ship	1968	350	650	1,200	1,200
MURRAY	Skipper	1968	350	650	1,200	1,200
MURRAY	Dolphin Gulf Stream	1968	350	650	1,200	1,200

Add $200 for original outboard motor

Manufacturer	Model or Style	Year	Fair	Good	CONDITION Excellent Original	Authentically Restored
PAL	Fire Chief	1949	150	250	750	600
PAL	Fire Dept.	1949	250	450	900	800
PAL	Torpedo Roadster	1949	300	500	1,000	1,000
STEGER	Fire Patrol	1948	400	600	1,200	1,200
STEGER	Station Wagon	1948	400	700	1,800	1,800
STEGER	Superamic	1948	600	900	2,000	2,000
STEELCRAFT	Buick	1924	2,400	3,200	5,500	5,500
STEELCRAFT	Chrysler	1925	3,000	4,000	7,500	6,500
STEELCRAFT	Stutz	1926	3,000	3,500	6,500	5,500
STEELCRAFT	Buick	1927	3,000	4,000	6,500	6,000
STEELCRAFT	Mack Truck	1929	3,000	3,500	6,500	5,500
STEELCRAFT	Nash	1929	1,800	2,800	5,500	5,500
STEELCRAFT	Packard	1932	4,500	5,500	10,000	8,500
STEELCRAFT	Pontiac	1932	2,000	2,500	4,000	4,000
STEELCRAFT	Chrysler	1933	3,500	5,000	9,000	7,500
STEELCRAFT	Chevrolet	1933	1,600	2,200	3,500	3,500
STEELCRAFT	2-Ton Mack	1935	1,000	2,000	4,000	3,500
STEELCRAFT	Lincoln	1935	3,200	4,000	7,500	6,000
STEELCRAFT	Air Mail	1935	3,000	3,800	6,000	5,500
STEELCRAFT	Airflow	1935	2,500	4,000	6,500	5,500
STEELCRAFT	Pontiac	1936	1,800	2,600	4,800	4,000
STEELCRAFT	Ace	1936	800	1,200	2,400	2,000

Manufacturer	Model or Style	Year	Fair	Good	CONDITION Excellent Original	Authentically Restored
STEELCRAFT	Sport Roadster	1935	1,500	2,000	3,500	3,000
STEELCRAFT	1-Ton Mack	1935	1,000	2,000	3,500	3,000
STEELCRAFT	Ford	1936	1,000	2,000	3,500	3,000
STEELCRAFT	Streamliner	1937	2,000	3,000	5,500	4,500
STEELCRAFT	Super Charger	1937	3,000	4,000	6,500	5,500
STEELCRAFT	Dodge	1941	1,200	1,600	3,200	2,800
STEELCRAFT	Buick	1941	2,000	2,500	4,000	4,000
STEELCRAFT	Spitfire	1941	1,500	2,000	3,500	3,500
TOLEDO	Hook & Ladder	1923	4,000	5,000	7,500	7,500
TOLEDO	Fire Chief	1923	3,500	4,500	6,500	6,500
TOLEDO	Willys-Knight	1923	4,000	5,000	8,500	8,500
TOLEDO	Jordan	1923	3,000	4,000	7,000	7,000
TOLEDO	Packard	1923	3,000	4,000	7,000	7,000
TOLEDO	Pierce-Arrow	1924	3,500	4,200	7,400	7,400
TOLEDO	Chrysler	1924	2,400	3,000	6,500	6,500
TOLEDO	Hudson	1925	2,000	2,800	4,200	4,200
TOLEDO	Lincoln	1931	3,000	4,000	7,500	6,500
TOLEDO	Pontiac	1932	2,000	2,800	4,000	4,000
TOLEDO	Buick	1933	2,400	3,200	4,500	4,500
TOLEDO	Tandem	1935	3,500	5,000	10,000	8,500
TOLEDO	Duesenberg Racer	1935	4,000	5,000	10,000	9,000
TOLEDO	Garford Truck	1935	3,000	4,000	6,500	5,500
TOLEDO	Skylark Airplane	1935	3,500	4,000	7,500	6,000
TOLEDO	Hupmobile	1936	3,000	3,600	5,000	4,500
TOLEDO	Auburn	1935	3,400	4,000	5,500	4,600
TOLEDO	Nash	1935	2,000	2,800	4,000	3,500
TOLEDO	Chrysler Airflow	1935	3,000	4,000	5,500	4,500
TOLEDO	DeSoto	1935	3,500	4,500	6,000	5,500
TOLEDO	Cadillac	1936	3,500	4,000	6,500	5,500
TOLEDO	Fire Dept.	1936	1,000	1,800	2,800	2,400
TOLEDO	G-Man Cruiser	1936	4,000	5,000	10,000	8,000
TOLEDO	Skippy Racer	1936	4,000	5,500	10,000	8,500
TRI-ANG	Vauxhall	1932	7,000	8,500	1,400	1,200
TRI-ANG	Rolls Royce	1930	10,000	14,000	20,000	20,000
TRI-ANG	Roadster	1934	2,500	3,200	5,000	5,000
TRI-ANG	Daimler	1938	7,500	9,000	12,000	12,000
TRI-ANG	Buick	1935	7,500	9,000	16,000	14,000
TRI-ANG	Race Car	1940	5,000	6,000	8,500	8,500
TRI-ANG	Racer	1948	1,200	2,000	3,500	3,500
TRI-ANG	Dump Truck	1950	375	500	1,200	1,000
TRI-ANG	Racer Super 8	1952	1,500	2,200	4,000	4,000
TRI-ANG	Station Wagon	1953	500	800	1,800	1,500
TRI-ANG	Centurion	1953	600	1,200	2,500	2,500
TRI-ANG	Prince	1953	200	450	750	750
TRI-ANG	Jeep	1953	600	800	2,000	1,800
TRI-ANG	Jaguar	1964–69	600	800	2,000	1,800

TRACTORS

Manufacturer	Model or Style	Year	Fair	Good	Excellent Original	Authentically Restored
ESKA	IH - Small H	1949	600	800	1,400	1,150
ESKA	IH - Large M	1950	750	800	1,250	1,000
ESKA	IH - 400	1954	400	600	1,000	800

Manufacturer	Model or Style	Year	Fair	Good	CONDITION Excellent Original	Authentically Restored
ESKA	IH - 450	1956	500	600	1,100	900
ESKA	IH - 560	1958	250	350	800	650
ERTL	IH - 806, 856, 1026	1963–70	175	200	600	450
ERTL	IH - 1066	1972	50	75	300	200
ERTL	IH - 1086	1978	50	75	300	200
ESKA	JD - Small 60	1952	300	600	1,200	900
ESKA	JD - Large 60	1955	400	600	1,200	900
ESKA	JD - 620	1956	400	600	1,000	800
ESKA	JD - 130	1958	500	600	1,200	900
ESKA	JD - 3 & 4 hole 10	1963	350	450	850	675
ERTL	JD - 20	1965	175	225	500	350
ERTL	JD - 30, 40, 50		50	75	275	225
ESKA	CASE - VAC	1953	700	800	1,500	1,400
ESKA	CASE - 400	1955	900	1,000	2,100	1,400
ESKA	CASE - 800	1958	700	800	1,200	1,000
ERTL	CASE - Pleasure King	1965	300	500	775	650
ERTL	CASE - 1070	1970	225	275	425	350
ESKA	AC - C	1949	550	650	1,100	800
ESKA	AC - CA	1950	600	800	1,400	1,000
ESKA	AC - D14	1957	600	700	1,200	1,000
ESKA	AC - D17	1958	600	700	1,200	1,000
ERTL	AC - 190	1966	400	500	700	650
ERTL	AC - 190 Bar Grill	1964	500	600	900	750
ERTL	AC - 200	1972	400	500	700	650
ERTL	AC - 7045	1978	200	300	450	400
ERTL	AC - 7080	1975	200	300	450	400
GRAPHIC	FORD - 900 & 901	1958	1,200	1,700	3,000	2,500
ERTL	FORD - 6000 Commander	1965	500	700	1,100	900
ERTL	FORD - 6000 Diesel	1963	1,000	1,500	3,500	2,700
	FORD - 8000		75	100	400	300
ESKA	MASSEY-HARRIS Large 44	1953	1,200	1,600	2,500	1,800
ERTL	MASSEY-FERGUSON 1105, 390 & 398		100	150	400	300
ESKA	OLIVER - Small 88	1947	1,000	1,200	2,200	1,800
ESKA	OLIVER - Super 88	1954	900	1,100	2,000	1,500
ESKA	OLIVER - 880	1958	700	850	1,800	1,200
ESKA	OLIVER - Cast Grill 1800	1962	1,200	1,600	2,800	2,000
ERTL	OLIVER - 1800, 1850, 1855	1963–72	400	500	1,000	750
ERTL	JD - Lawn & Garden		250	300	750	550

INDEX